Prison Mom
How to have peace when your world is turned upside down

Demetria Williams

Cover Design: ZMARS Design
Edited by Elijah Jean Editing.

Some names and identifying details have been changed to protect the privacy of individuals. I have tried to recreate events, locales and conversations from my memories of them. In order to maintain their anonymity in some instances I have changed the names of individuals and places, I may have changed some identifying characteristics and details such as physical properties, occupations and places of residence. Some names and identifying details have been changed and or omitted to protect the privacy of individuals.

DEDICATION

This book is dedicated to my four beautiful children who I love and cherish so much. To Elijah, my loving son and whom I see great potential in. Elijah, you are my melody to my tune. I love you with a *never-ending* love. I want you to know one thing; I see what you are going through. I want you to know that I continue to pray for you daily and that we will make it through this dark time. Elijah, I want you to take what God has put in you and use it to lead others down a different path. I believe in you son. You were made to be different.

To Anijah, my only daughter and my *best friend*, I love you sweetheart. Anijah you are my heart beat. I want you to always remember that you are beautiful, very special and very smart. God made you for a special purpose. You are unique; so be the leader God called you to be. Don't follow the crowd, instead, lead it baby girl. I wait patiently to see you on the platform God has prepared for you.

Tony, you are my shelter during the rain; the spitting image of myself. Son, you remind me so much of myself. I was just like you growing up. I was a leader but I found myself in places I didn't want to be. Yet, in all those places God used me in ways I couldn't imagine. I love you son and I will never give up on you. Tony, I want you to know that you don't belong in jail. I know that it seems strange what you are going through but I want you to know that you have a strong calling on your life. Son, I will see you on the outside soon. I will be waiting with my arms stretched wide as the sea.

Danny, my loving first born, whom I admire so much, you are everything to me! You are my sunshine on a rainy day. Son, you have a heart that's bigger than this world. You are caught up in a strange situation; you don't belong in jail. You belong out here spreading your love because people need to know love. But I can say God has a special purpose for you son. I love you and I will be waiting by the gate on your out date with my arms stretched wide as the sea. Danny, I will *never* give up on you.

PROLOGUE

I thank God for setting me free from my very own prison – my mind. When I first started writing this book I wasn't being honest with my readers or myself. Instead of fully sharing my story, I kept certain parts hidden. The devil made me believe that if I told my story, people would make fun of me and would look at me as weak. I was held hostage to the lies that he placed in my mind. So, in my heart, I kept a journal, locking it away for no one to read. I never had any intention to ever release that journal. I was going to take all the information it held, all the unspoken words, to the grave.

I was tired of feeling worthless and invisible. Writing this book no longer fulfilled a purpose. In fact, I was simply writing so I could say that I wrote another book. For years, I felt abandoned. I was tired of feeling alone or like I didn't exist. Because of this, I did everything in my power to be noticed by someone – anyone. I went to college hoping my family or friends would give me praise. I wrote two books before this one to get my name out in the world as a famous author. I was so messed up in my mind from the devils lies that I truly believed that all of these things would bring me recognition, but they didn't. All they did was give me temporary gratification. I was still in prison inside.

I wanted to be recognized. It was a hard realization, but I knew in order for me to truly tell my story, I had to let go of the things that were holding me. It took time, a lot of tears, a lot of heartache and a lot of patience. However, without that journey I would have been unable to provide you, my readers, with Prison Moms. But most importantly without the support of my family and friends I would not have the strength to carry on and finish.

INTRODUCTION

Across the world today, many mothers have found themselves in unforeseen situations, which unexpectedly appears in their lives. For these mothers', in a matter of moments their whole world is turned upside down. Destroyed by the tragedy and reality that no mother ever wants to face—their child(children) receiving an adult sentence and sent to an adult prison to carry out years of imprisonment. There are even children who are sentenced to life without the possibility of Parole. Like a tsunami, sentences like these hit hard—causing extreme destruction while destroying everything in its path. It comes out of nowhere with very little or no warning at all and leaves very little time to map an escape plan. Yet this tsunami, involves you and your children. It is nearly impossible to survive something as devastating as the "tsunami" which may come in your life such as losing your children to prison.

A mother that has lost her children to prison may suffer psychological problems which can last for days, years or an entire life time. *Prison Mom's* — mothers whose children were taken from them and sent to prison — suffer from grief and depression. Some, if not most, are left feeling guilty and even blame themselves for their child's prison sentence. Others are angry with the justice system. And often many of these women are single mother's. With little resources, available to turn to, these mothers are sometimes left with no hope and feel all alone. Having your child in prison is not easy; I know this firsthand.

As you continue reading this book you are about to step into the world — a mother who didn't lose one of her children to prison, but two. In this book, I will be sharing my life with you and my unfinished journey of being a Prison Mom. I know the devastation you are going through because I am living through it. I understand the heartache, the confusion and the desperation that comes with wanting your child home. But I know that prison started for my kids before the judge sentence them. It started in their minds and that is what lead them behind prison bars; Just like he held me hostage in my mind for years, he did the same to my children. But God is setting them free just like he did for me. My two boys are my world, and the worst feeling is to have is your world taken away

Yet, I am here to share a story of hope and healing. I want you to know that there is still hope in the midst of a hopeless situation. Through my very own experiences I learned that the world breaks everyone: the very good, the very gentle, the brave, and the ones who trust God. Understand this, there is no shame in being a broken person because with the help of God you can pick up the pieces and start building something brand new and whole.

Before I go any further, I will like to ask you some questions. Can you think of a time when you felt like, what in the world is going on in my life? Why did that happen to me? When will I finally get what I've wanted for so long? Why God, why this happen to me? If you've been alive very long, you've probably had an experience like this at some point. The truth is God loves us and He has good plans for our lives but it doesn't mean life is always easy.

We all go through difficult times and things happen that aren't fair. In fact, Jesus tells us in John 16:33, "In the world you have tribulation and trials and distress and frustration." It's so important for us to understand this so we won't be confused and lose our faith in Him when life is hard. Thankfully, Jesus goes on to say, "But be of good cheer take courage; be confident, certain, undaunted. For I have overcome the world.

I have deprived it of power to harm you and conquered it for you" (yes your situation). This is amazing assurance through Christ that everything is going to work out the way it should in the end. I know firsthand what it's like to hurt so much that you're not sure you can stand it any longer or survive because the pain is so unbearable.

There have been times when I didn't understand how God could allow me to go through some of the things I've went through. There were many days and nights that I prayed to God asking him to please rescue me by taking me to heaven with him because I was so tired of pain. I tried to figure out how to fix my problems but it was so difficult for me.

Today I can say that I no longer look for a reason in my mind but I know that God is with me and all the bad I faced, God is working it out for my good. Now I know that my pain is used for a great purpose. Despite the bad things, I can also say that God did a lot of good things in my life. He has been using me to help others to know that with Him you can make it through anything life throws at you. One thing I have learned is that God can restore you from devastating situations. He can give you peace right during a storm and keep you filled with joy. Through the devastation I endured, I learned how to trust God when I didn't understand and how to release my faith during trials.

God wants us to come to a place in our relationship with Him where we trust that He's in control and He has our best interest at heart even when our situation doesn't seem fair. He wants us to rest and have peace that surpasses our understanding in every circumstance we face because then, and only then will we be mentally and emotionally stable. That way, we won't be driven by our feelings and become fearful and discouraged. I can truly say that God is using me in ways that I never dreamed of. He didn't cause the bad things in my life but He did allow me to go through them. He knew that one day he was going to use all the bad that happen to me for my good. And He is doing just that. What the devil meant for my harm, God is using it for my good.

1

I grew up in Peoria, Illinois a small city with a population of about 116,513. I was raised in a Christian household with Christian values along with six siblings. Back then, it was not common to have both parents living together so I felt very blessed and lucky to have them both with me. Having both parents under the same roof was like living my very own fairy tale—I just knew one day I would have my very own happily ever after.

One of my favorite past times were our family dinners because I loved being able to spend time together. As the king of his castle, my dad sat at the head of the table while my mom—as the beautiful queen she was—sat at the other end of the table on her throne. My parents were accompanied by my six siblings, including myself, at a big oak wood dining room table that my dad kept polished and spotless. However, when we sat down as a family to eat, that spotless table quickly changed its appearance.

With all the pigging out we did, it went from spotless to full of spots. My dad always made sure our stomachs were packed and full with whatever he put on our plate. We couldn't leave that table until our plates were clean — we had to eat everything. He made sure we were satisfied before we stepped away from the table.

My dad was my super hero. He made sure we never went without even if that meant making some bad choices to provide for us. At the time, he wasn't concerned about the consequences behind his choices. All he was concerned about was providing for his family. Although he made some bad choices, I didn't see them as *bad* because my eyes were occupied with all the luxury things my dad did for my family and I. He made sure we were in the nicest home with the nicest furniture. All I ever saw was my daddy bending over backwards to make sure our lights turned on when we flicked the switch, he made sure we kept food on the table and clothes on our back. My dad was the greatest daddy in the world to me and he still is today.

My mom was a beautiful woman. She had a mocha caramel skin complexion and had the shape of coke bottle. Her big brown piercing eyes captivated anyone who looked into them. Her hair was like silk and kept in a short cut.

For the life of me I don't see why she wasn't on the front cover of a magazine—she deserved to be because her beauty was like no other. God took his time when he created my mom. Her beauty was rare. He gave her the type of curves every woman desires—small at the top, small waist, and curvy hips with a nice rear. My mom had a beautiful face that pulled along a beautiful body. But, it wasn't just her outer beauty, her inner beauty was just as rare. My mom had a loving heart and a gentle spirit. She often put her family before her own needs making sure that we well taken care of.

She made many sacrifices for her family and that included giving up everything to be a stay home mom. She was a meek woman who was full of grace. When I would look at her, I found myself desiring the lifestyle she was living. All she had to do was look pretty, and she didn't have to work hard doing it. It came natural for her because God graced her with it. But that wasn't all God gave her; he blessed her with the gift of culinary arts. That woman could cook anything.

I remember during the holidays the scent of her food was the most pleasant smell that entered my nostrils. My nostrils would be filled with the aroma of fresh collard greens and juices from a big turkey my mom had cooking along with the other foods that were being cooked on the stove and in the oven. Those delicious smells always dragged my body right to the kitchen to sneak a bite of whatever my mom was cooking. She never knew because I went in when she stepped out, and I was out of the kitchen by the time she came back. I would run out so fast you would think I was a track star; I'm surprised that I wasn't recognized for my 200 meters. I should've been rewarded with a piece of turkey for how fast I would run out of the kitchen. These were some of the best memories of my childhood.

Then one day it all fell apart. It was as if my fairy tale turned into a nightmare and my loving memories turned into tragedies. I'm not sure when it happened, but one day I looked up and realized my dad was gone. When he left, so did my happily ever after; it was replaced with tales from the crypt. My life became dark. I felt abandoned by my super hero. Still, to this day, I do not know why my parents separated.

Had I known, I would've done everything in my little bitty power to restore my 'happily ever after' and bring my mom and dad back together. By then, it was too late. My parents already grew apart and even as a child I saw the distance in their hearts. My dad moved on with his life and when he left my happiness left along with him. Even though he wasn't living at home, he was still a great father and we all missed him.

I missed going to church together and having family meals together. It was strange that he wasn't there anymore. During this time, I was angry with both of my parents. I was so angry with them for taking away my happily ever after. When they separated, they snatched my only piece of happiness away from me. My mom was no longer my dad's rib; instead, it felt as though God took her out his side and made her his ex. They didn't think about how I felt about their separation. I always loved my mother but when the separation happened I latched onto my dad, both in my mind and heart. When I would daydream about living with him my heart would leap with happiness. However, it was all just a fantasy, the dream never became real. Despite this truth, I never abandoned my fantasy.

Now, without dad in the home, it was up to my mom to raise all six of us. Although my father still provided for us, my mother did a good job raising us. Later down the line, I noticed my mom's stomach expanding. I soon found out that she was carrying twin boys. My happily ever after drew further and further away — eight kids and a single mother.

Our little box apartment went from holding a soccer team to a mass choir. Years later, my youngest brother (after the twins) made his grand entrance causing our mass choir to expand even more. At first, it was fun having everyone in the house because it was never a dull moment with all of us; however, it all changed when my sister and I were forced to be a nanny to our younger siblings. At the time we were young teens. And although we loved our younger siblings, we didn't have a clue of what we were doing when we cared for them. Yet as time went on, more responsibilities were added—my mom would have us cooking and cleaning daily. My mom was a neat freak. If she saw a spot on the kitchen floor, she would wake us up out of our sleep to clean it. It was as if we were working graveyard shifts.

My happily ever after finally left my mind. It walked out on me and went to some other little girls' home while I was left with heavy loads to carry on my little shoulders. Here I was in a child's body, yet, doing grown woman things. I went from playing kick ball to holding the ball of responsibilities. We had to do so much that we didn't have time to play outside with the neighborhood kids. I couldn't take it, so in my mind I started to create an escape plan. I saw myself running away from home, chasing my happily ever after but the more I was chasing it the faster it got. Before I knew it, my happily ever after disappeared, leaving me in the wind, wrapped up with grown woman responsibilities. During these times, I felt all alone and worn out from the heavy task my mother had put on me. I was no longer living my fairytale. What I didn't know was that my nightmares just began.

2

After my parent's separation, I developed abandonment and trust issues. I felt like a little girl who was left in a vacant apartment by her parents. I was afraid, scared and angry. My heart was like an icebox; it was cold and hard. I always was under the impression that when you are married you are together forever, but my mother and father proved me wrong. For the first time, my dad broke my heart. He was my best friend and protector, yet he abandoned me. What was worse, it seemed when he left, I was left with the load he should've carried. I had so much anger towards them for separating. The separation hurt yet, later down the road when they got a divorce it made things worse. A small part of me was still hoping for restoration. I think that is where it all started. I was so angry with them because our little perfect family was ripped apart how hurricane Katrina ripped apart New Orleans.

Prison Mom

To my horror, the nightmare didn't stop there. At a young tender age I was being molested by a family member. This man took my most precious possession. He took my choice to choose when he took my virginity. He was a thief in the night and a gigolo in the day time; he always had a lot of girls swinging on his coat tail. Yet, it never stopped him from *playing house* with me when everyone was sound asleep or when family was sitting out in the backyard of my grandma house. During those times, I was being stripped of my self-worth, my hope, and even my desire to live. My uncle should have protected me but instead he was destroying me.

At the time, I blamed my mother for this because he was her brother and she left him to babysit my siblings and I. I also blamed my father for leaving me behind when he packed up and left. Although I blamed both my parents, most of the blame was towards my mom for letting this person baby sit her girls. She never knew or had a clue that I blamed her because I kept it all bottled inside. I was so angry with my mom because at the time, I felt like she was feeding me to the wolves every time she let this person baby sit. For years, I hoped one day it would all disappear and things would go back to normal. It didn't. As I grew up, it got worse.

Being molested damaged me in ways no one could ever imagine, unless it happened to them. My whole life spiraled out of control. I was facing the wrong direction being lead down a dark road. I felt unworthy, unloved, lost, and abandoned. There were days I just wanted to lie down and never wake up because the pain was unbearable. There were even days when I contemplated suicide. I wanted to check out of this world and believed suicide was the only way to end this pain. I just knew if I died, I would escape the pain I was battling within my mind and inside of me. For years, I fought with the demons I carried in my mind and heart. Yet, for years they terrorized me and lead me into darker situations.

I was in so much pain, that I found myself in many unhealthy relationships. But at the time I didn't see these relationships as unhealthy. Instead they "helped" to take the pain away. I felt accepted and I felt loved. It was like I was rescued from my abandonment. However, this was short lived. Because even though I felt this way, it wasn't real. It was a false sense of hope. After these relationships, I would still feel unworthy, ashamed and lost. I became so angry with God. I wanted to know why He let something like this happen to me. I was so coldhearted and became so selfish that I even asked God "Why didn't you let this happen to one of my other sisters?" For years, I asked God this question amongst many others and received no answer. The more silent he became the more rage that boiled inside of me.

Prison Mom

I didn't want anything to do with God. My anger took over and I started becoming rebellious. I started running away from home and hanging out at my friend's house. My escape plan that I previously mapped out began to unfold. When my mom came looking for me, I would hide out and tell my friends to tell her, they haven't seen me. I made my friends into little O.J. Simpsons — I had them lying and covering for me because I didn't want to go home to deal with grown women responsibilities. I just wanted to have fun as a young girl. I wanted to attend parties, have sleepovers', and I wanted to see what it was like to stay out after the street lights came on. All I wanted to do was have a normal life like every child deserves to have. I just wanted to belong. So, I did anything I could do to feel normal.

When I was 15, I joined a gang called *Gangster Disciples.* All we ever did was fight other gangs. Every day, it was like I was in Iraq fighting a war. One time, I was stabbed under my eye. To this day, I still have that scar. Doing these things were wrong but at the time I didn't see it this way. What I saw was belonging. When I was with my gang members, I felt like I was adopted into a family — we were together every day. We shared clothes, money and even rooms wherever we laid our heads at that night. I was doing just about anything to try to cope with the pain I was dealing with inside but my friends never knew because I kept it all bottled inside. I made sure to keep a tight lid on my pain.

One particular night, my friends and I paid this lady to use her car to go out on the town. We planned on having the time of our life. That night we ended up going to a night club called Scorpio's. It was a little box club that sat on the corner of Jefferson—a busy street in Peoria Many of us weren't even old enough to get in the club but the doorman never knew because we used someone else's ID and we all dressed and had personalities of grown women, so it was easy to deceive him. We danced the night away. Since the night was still young, we decided to leave the club and drive to the Northside of Peoria to stalk the house of some Chicago man that one of my friends had relations with. When we arrived, the man that my friend was dating, was standing outside of his apartment with another lady, and from the looks of it they were enjoying each other's presence. They looked like they were standing underneath a mistletoe on a cold winter night. My girlfriend saw this and became very aggressive and out control. Seeing this made her very upset. We continued circling the block and upon that last time circling I noticed a gun in this gentleman hand. When I saw the gun, I knew we were about to face a gun battle unarmed. It was war time for us.

I informed everyone in the car but they all thought I was joking. Amid warning the crew, we all heard the first shots fired. I quickly ducked my head to keep a bullet from going through my skull. That night, my life flashed before my eyes as I heard about twelve or more shots fire. The bullets were flying and took every window out in the car while my friend who was driving, tried to steer the car while on the floor to get us away. She drove across one of the busiest streets in Peoria. Losing control of the car and not being able to see, she ended up crashing into a utility pole. Luckily, we were all able to get out; so, we all jumped out and started running away. While running, we ran right into a police officer. The police officer then went to the crime scene to apprehend the man with the happy trigger finger. However, no arrest was made because the man disappeared like a thief in the night. It seemed he disappeared so fast that he didn't even leave a piece of lint from his pant pocket behind to link him to his crime he had committed. The police later told us that we were lucky to be alive because one of the bullets hit an inch away from the gas tank, which didn't have a gas cap on. The car was totaled, yet, beside some shattered glass cuts, we all walked out safe.

It would seem that night would have taught me a lesson; it didn't. I couldn't control the feelings I had inside so I continued down this dark road because I thought there was no hope for me. Plus, no one acted concern. To everyone I was just another bad child who would end up dead before the age of 21.

Sad thing is, one day I thought their assumptions would be right and I was going to be on the front page of the newspaper as a homicide victim.

One summer on Saturday night around 1:30pm, my friends and I decided to pile up into a two-door car to travel to Decatur from Peoria to go out to a club. The next day, on our way back, the car went completely dead. We were on the highway, in the middle of nowhere between Decatur and Peoria, about 84 miles away from home. We were stranded, scared and hopeless and stood out there with no clue of how we were going to get home. Cell phones weren't popular at that time so we didn't have any way to call anyone. We stood out there for about twenty-five minutes. While we stood hopeless, an older Caucasian man who was driving by stopped and told us that we could stay the night at his house and he would fix our car tomorrow. Everyone said no way. That didn't sound right, and although we were young we could tell when things were off.

After hours of being stranded, a younger African man stopped and offered us a ride. He told us that he would get us as close to Peoria as he could. Although we were scared, we got in his car because we were tired and ready to get home. As he was driving down the highway we noticed he was wearing black gloves and was tightly gripping the steering wheel. The way he gripped that wheel was suspicious. His look was stern and he said nothing.

Prison Mom

We all began to have doubts, thinking maybe we should not have gotten in the car. The way he gripped the steering wheel looked as if he wanted to choke the life out of someone. Honestly, he scared us; so, we took off our shoes to use as a weapon if he tried anything. I was wearing brown ankle boots with six inch heels. They were thick heels but it didn't matter, all that mattered to me at the time was how I was going to protect myself. We kept our seatbelts off just in case we had to jump out and run. He must have sensed our fear because as he let us out in East Peoria at a gas station he informed us that he was a minister. We were in complete shock. Although we didn't understand it then, it was shocking to see how much God cared for us that night and many nights after. I knew God was with us, yet, we still gave in to living in the streets and doing things our own ways. We were lost souls with no sense of direction.

3

Years later, I met a man from Chicago who was down in Peoria handling some drug operations. He worked around the clock and I didn't like it. He would be on the block selling drugs instead of spending time with me. Although he was a drug dealer, I cared deeply for him. Months later I became pregnant with my oldest son. I was nervous and scared because I was a baby carrying a baby. I was only seventeen years old with no clue of how to be a mother. Despite this, it didn't stop me or his father from being excited. We couldn't wait to have our baby and start our very own little family together. Here I was, seventeen and pregnant; my emotions were in an uproar, filled with happiness and excitement. For the first time in a long time, I felt like I found my happily-ever-after. I was going to have a family.

That excitement quickly turned to tears and a broken heart when my child's father was viciously gunned down and killed in the streets of Peoria. It was during my third month while carrying our baby. Again, my happily-ever-after was stripped away, but this time it left me in the dark without a flashlight and without an urge to live. I was angry and hurt; my heart was shattered into millions of broken pieces. The one person I was planning a life with was taken away from me and my child's life. It felt unreal and I was devastated. Every time things were getting better for me, my little piece of happiness would be snatched away and because of this, I didn't want to live anymore. All hope was lost.

I was at a place of no return and my world kept spinning out of control. I didn't care about anything. Throughout my pregnancy I would heavily be involved in gang fights. I was very angry and emotional yet did my best to hide it and pretend that I was ok. I felt abandoned, so I searched for someone to rescue me from my misery. Out of nowhere my search stopped.

I met the lucky guy; he was a tall, handsome black man with long hair that embraced his strong shoulders. I fell head over heels. He made me feel like I was worth something and made me feel like life was worth living. I felt rescued from all the pain I was carrying. By this time, I had my baby. He was so nice and caring and treated my baby boy like he was his own.

Before I knew it, months later after we started dating and got serious, I ended up with a bun in the oven—I was pregnant with my second child. I was on a high, excited again because I was going to be sharing a child with a man that I loved and that said he loved me. He promised that he would never leave me to raise this child alone—I believed him, and trusted him. I was in love and happy.

That happiness was short lived. The caring and loving I received disappeared and was replaced with black eyes and busted lips. Name calling became part of my daily life, and each day it became worse and worse. The more I endured the more pain was added to my fragile heart. I felt unworthy. I was only nineteen years old dealing with all his nonsense. I tried but I couldn't escape this pain. So, I did what I knew best, I continued down this dead-end road crying out for help.

My voice was the loudest on that dark lonely road. My destructive behavior was my call out for attention but no one heard me. Because I was known to be rebellious, everyone just thought I was just another disobedient child. What they didn't understand was that I was a hurting child. The saying goes "hurting people, hurt people" yet, my family never saw my hurt. If they did, they didn't try to bandage my wounds with their love. I had nowhere to turn so, I stayed with him. When I stayed, the abuse got worse.

Prison Mom

Now, I know you're probably asking why I didn't leave; I did. I separated from this person many times with the intention of never returning. The first time I left, I was so afraid of the unknown that I quickly turned back to the familiar chaos, hoping things would be different, but the abuse got worse. I stayed in this unhealthy relationship because he would always come running back to me. When he did this, I felt needed and like someone cared about me. I was under the strong delusion that we were love birds. But we were not. We were caught up in the lust and false love. Neither one of use knew what true love was.

The second time I called it the quits was because I was tired of looking in the mirror and facing a black ring around my eye. Despite this, like the first time, I returned to him once again. This cycle continued and I would take him back many times. He always promised to never hit me again, but it was a lie. Every time he cried his heart out, and his lips sang "I'm sorry, I won't hit you again", I believed him. I came to find out they weren't real tears; it was the Seagram's gin he would drink before coming out of his eyes. I was tired, and my heart was broken from so much pain. After all the lies, I had enough and I made up in my mind to leave and to leave for good.

One night I decided to take my boys to a relative house to go to a house party with a very close girlfriend of mine. We both looked so beautiful. We looked like we were in a fashion show, that's how sharp we were dressed. My hair was banging that night. It was long and silky and hung past my shoulders. Excited, I thought I was on my way to dance the night away. I didn't know this night would become a near death experience for me.

That night, the man that proclaimed that he would never hit me again, stabbed me multiple times and left me for dead. He took a knife and stabbed me in my stomach. When that wasn't good enough for him, he took the knife out of my stomach and stabbed me in my lower back. He was cutting me like a butcher cutting a deer. It was clear he wanted me dead. Wanting to finish me off, he tried pulling the knife out my lower back, however, the only part that came out was the handle. The blade didn't want to leave my flesh; it had a tight grip on my lower back. At that moment, I thought my pain was finally over.

I was ready to die and leave all my pain behind for my family to deal with. But God wasn't ready for me to die. That is what my father told me as he was standing by my hospital bed praying. I laid there on a life support machine fighting for my life.

I was tired of pain so that day I hoped for the doctors to let me die. Then suddenly an image flashed before me—it was my two little boys. At that moment, I knew I had to live for my babies. I knew that my babies needed me more than anything so I put on my boxing gloves and started fighting to live. I was ducking and diving every time it seemed like my heart was going to quit on me. I stayed in that ring until the doctors said it was okay for me to go home.

4

Years later

I separated from the man that stabbed me and later down the line I started dating a gentleman that seemed like he was different from the rest. He took me on dates and treated me like I was the only woman on this earth. There was nothing he wouldn't do for me. He loved my kids like they were his very own. In the beginning, things were so great for our little family that we ended up moving in a house together. And eventually, years later I had two kids by this gentleman—a son and a daughter who were four years apart. Once again, I thought I found my happily-ever-after. Everything was going well for our family until the cheating and fighting started. And boy did we fight but I wasn't having it this time around. I had made up in my mind that there's no way another man was going to hit me and get away with it.

I told him that if he ever raised his hands at me that he was going to lose them. He didn't believe me, and tried to hit me, so I stabbed him. I was fed up. Although unsuccessful, I tried to cut his hands off, I didn't care if he could never use his hands again. Like clockwork, after all the fighting was over we would go back to our romantic moments. We would go to fancy restaurants and sit down and eat; go to movies just so I could cuddle in his arms or we would go to a night club just to showcase our dancing skills. It was toxic, but I loved the romantic moments.

While dating this man my younger sons' — Tony — father was gunned down in the streets of Peoria. His killer shot him in the back of his head. My sons heart was broken because my son loved his dad. When this happened, I felt cursed. I felt like everything I touched was vanishing from off the earth.

I attended the funeral with the company of my best friend, Love. While there, the preacher spoke about salvation. He preached so good that he pricked our hearts. For the first time in a long time someone could climb the wall I had built in my life. I had my guards up so far above my head that I am surprised it didn't scare the pastor off. I knew it didn't because he was long winded with his message. He didn't give up. It was like he knew what I needed that day.

It was as if God told him "Demetria will be at this funeral so I need you to climb that wall she has built to keep me out and get to the heart of the matter." God was correct because I was angry. I was angry with God for letting all the bad things happen in my life. But after the preachers' message, I made an agreement with Love, that we were going to attend church that following Sunday.

We were so tired of hurting and living our life without God. We were tired of people rejecting us. We were tired of feeling like orphans. Our lives were lonely and hopeless. At that time in our life, it was like we were living on a different planet because we had nobody in our life that cared for us. So, that following Sunday we attended Love's mother-in-law church.

We were like ants in the church because it was packed with all sorts of people. We saw women with big fancy hats that made bold statements, traveling around the church like they owned it. However, those same hats blocked some of the congregations' view. I knew they couldn't even see the pastor in his suit. He was sharp that day; it looked like he had his suit tailor made just to fit his little short statue. During the sermon, I heard some noises behind me as I sat down in my chair after devotion. It came from some boys lusting after my round apple shape butt. They were drooling at the mouth like thirsty hound dogs.

They made me feel so uncomfortable because they were undressing me with their binoculars that sat below their forehead and above their nose. The Pastors message couldn't even stop them from talking about my back end. It was a mess. The Pastor motioned the congregation to stand up and gave the altar call. When he gave the call, we both ran to the altar so fast that we almost knocked each other down. You would've have sworn that Love and I were running marathon.

Before he could start the plan of salvation we told him that we wanted to accept Jesus Christ into our hearts as our Savior. We said it like the world was about to end and Jesus was returning to rapture his people. We were ready for Jesus to rapture us from the dark road we were traveling down because nobody else could save us.

That day Love and I dedicated our life *back* to Christ. Yes, I said 'back to Christ' because once upon a time in our life we had made Him our Savior; but when the storms started appearing in our life we didn't want anything to do with him. Do you know God later revealed to me that he never did leave me nor forsake me. I tried to do things my way so he allowed me to make my own choices while he waited patiently because he was not going to force his way on me. He showed me, at that moment, that I have a choice; I could do it alone or with him.

I really thought, in my crowded mind, that I could live my life without Jesus but I was proved wrong over and over again.

Immediately after I got saved I started being judgmental as if I was perfect. That judgment started right in my home. It was like my kids and my boyfriend were in court every morning the moment they rose from their beds. The only difference from a judge and I was the robe.

I didn't wear a robe but I wore ignorance as my clothing and a blindfold on my eyes. No one ever told us what salvation really was, and this church was very judgmental. Sunday after Sunday they preached a demanding, angry, judgmental God. Then I would go home and preach this same sermon every day to my kids, family and boyfriend because I started believing the lies. It was so bad that my kids, family, and boyfriend didn't want anything to do with God. They were tired of me cramming God down their throats and slapping them upside their head like a bible stomper. They were tired of me quoting scriptures every time they made mistakes and they were tired of me thinking that I was better than them because I attended church every Sunday and they didn't. I remember my boyfriend asking me "What's the use of you going to church if you is mean as hell?"

Here I was thinking I was saved but all along I was still lost. I was lost from the truth yet "saved" by a whole bunch of rules that I couldn't keep, even though I was trying to get everyone else to keep them. I remember telling Love that I felt like I was an Israelite when they were in the Egypt with Pharaoh, I was treated like a Hebrew Slave.

I felt alone and lost. I wasn't getting spiritually fed in the church. I was getting beat down Sunday after Sunday with harsh teaching. I felt like I did when I was with an abusive controlling man.

All I ever heard in church was "You can't". You can't do this or you can't do that. Although this church was my choice, I felt like I was being forced to keep rules that only Jesus was able to keep because *He's* perfect, I'm not! (But through him and only him I am made in his image.) I never heard or understood what Jesus done for me. If I did hear anything good about Him, it was that He died and rose from the dead. That was the only *good news* I was hearing; the rest was bad news. I tried so hard to be perfect because I was afraid if I made a mistake that God was going to punish me or send me straight to hell. This is what the pastor was preaching. He was tearing me apart like a lion tears apart their prey. I was bleeding inside from all the painful wounds I was carrying, and the words sliced me deeper. Despite this, these wounds didn't stop me from trying to be perfect because I was afraid to mess up.

The more I tried the more I messed up, but it never stopped me from trying to change my imperfect self. I never had a clue that change was so simple because this pastor made it so hard for me.

My kids caught hell with me; it was as if they were walking in hell with gasoline draws on. They were walking on egg shells. They had to walk a straight narrow line and couldn't make any mistakes in my eyesight. I was an angry drill sergeant. Even though I attended church every Sunday I was still an angry bitter, black woman. I was full of so much pain and rage; going to church didn't take any of it away. In fact, it added on to my pain because the man who stood on the pulpit Sunday after Sunday reminded me of an abusive controlling man. He would proudly stand on that platform and beat us down with his judgmental message. Instead of him feeding the sheep, he was beating us. I was striving so hard to please a Holy God but it never worked. The more I tried to please God the worse I got. Because of this, my pain never went away, as a matter of fact it got worse.

5

I continued attending church but I started my search for a new one because I couldn't take any more beatings from that man who stood on the pulpit. After some time, I eventually left that church and joined another. I joined a church where the people seem a little different. I saw smiles every Sunday when I was greeted at the door by the greeters. My kids and I attended church every time the church doors were open. It was like we lived at the church instead of at home because we spent more time there than at home.

At the time, I had two other children, Anijah and Elijah, a total of four children who was following along behind their broken mother. My children were only allowed to go to school, church and home. Doing this, I truly thought I was protecting my children. I was doing everything in my power to keep my kids from going through any type of pain and to keep them from ever feeling the way I was feeling inside. I was damaged inside and I didn't think I could be repaired. I tried everything to keep my kids from being damaged, not realizing that I was adding pain to their life by smoldering them.

I had my children tucked so tightly in my pouch that they were suffocating. I sheltered my daughter and held her so close to my heart. I was protecting her like I wished my mom would've done me as a child.

On the other hand, with my boys I had a brick wall in between us. I treated them as if they were the one who had molested me. I was so afraid and scared from what my uncle did that I made my boys suffer for his crime. I wasn't intentionally doing this but I couldn't stop because I didn't know how to control it. Despite this, I still tried to keep my kids in this little "perfect" bubble. I thought I was in right standing with God by doing this but I wasn't. I was in right standing with the devil and didn't even know it (John 10:10).

My children had a rough child hood yet I truly thought that I was providing them with the best child hood. I even acted this way towards my boyfriend at the time. I acted as if he was some kind of disease and I was better than him because I was going to church and he wasn't. At the time, I had no clue of God's mercy. I thought you had to do everything in your power to please God and boy did I try. I was so stressed out and wore out from trying to please a Holy God in my filthy sinful flesh it seemed impossible. The more I tried the more I failed. But I still thought I was better than my boyfriend because I was attending church and he wasn't.

Years later, I decided to be kept until marriage and give up on having sex. I didn't want any more babies out of wedlock, I wanted a husband. My boyfriend didn't understand this. As a matter fact, I didn't either. At the time, I didn't care about what he understood. I just wanted my body to be kept from sex until I was married. It didn't work in the beginning; I failed many times because my attempt to keep myself was no good at all. The more I tried to say no to my boyfriend, the more my flesh said yes. We continued this way for about a year until I prayed and asked God to keep my body until marriage. It was *really* hard for us because we shared the same house and the same bed and on most nights, we slept in our birthday suits.

The sex didn't stop until I started sleeping on the couch. I realized that no human being on this earth can be kept while lying in the bed every night together cuddled up with their birthday suits on. No, I am not saying that God is weak, I am saying that our flesh is very weak. No matter how hard you try in your self-efforts, it won't work.

At the time my boyfriend thought I was cheating because I was no longer having sex with him. I figured if he called it cheating because I was on my couch spending more time communicating with God and praying than with him, then so be it. We ended up separating because of that.

His flesh still wanted sex and I wanted to be kept by God until marriage. Each day, after he left home, before our separation, he was in bed with another woman. When he walked out on our relationship I was hurting. Not only because he cheated, but because we called off our wedding which we already started paying money on. Yes, I said wedding. In the midst of everything, he proposed to me. He wanted so badly to make things work between us but he couldn't because his flesh wanted something different than his heart. His flesh wanted sex but his heart wanted me as a wife. So, we called it off.

I felt abandoned for the millionth time. It felt like I was going to lose my mind, all I was missing at that time was a strait jacket and a padded room. The rejection was unbearable. I couldn't bear being without this man because I was afraid to be alone; every time someone walked out of my life my abandonment issues become worse. I just couldn't take it any longer so I decided to move out of Peoria, Illinois and moved to Decatur, Illinois with my father. I moved there to try to dodge the pain and also because I didn't want to end up back into my boyfriend's arms because I knew he didn't change. I knew I was weak and vulnerable and if I stayed I would end up right back in an unhealthy relationship with him even though the cheating got worse. He was on a rampage with his promiscuous lifestyle and I didn't want that any more. I wanted healing so bad that I was craving for it just like a drug addict craves for his or her fix.

My dad was very happy that I decided to pack up my things to come and stay with him but my kids and I weren't. We were hurting. We were taken out of our comfort zone to enter the unknown. We left the only family they had ever known to be with my dad. Although I was around my dad at a younger age, after my mom and his separation, he moved back to Decatur where most of his family resided. I thought I was running from my pain by leaving Peoria. I truly thought I could out run it or leave it with my ex.

Never realizing that my pain was running with me because I was hurting so bad inside from all I had been through. Many nights, I cried a river to God telling Him that I just wanted to be loved. I was so broken. I didn't feel loved; I didn't feel worthy and I didn't feel like living. When my ex got a new girlfriend, I felt betrayed, rejected and forgotten. He didn't take any time auditioning for a woman to fill that role.

There were nights when I would lay awake thinking about suicide. I thought suicide was the only way to end my pain. No one never knew because I pretended everything was alright. I kept this act up half of my entire life. I was afraid to tell people that I was hurting because I thought that they would look at me different.

I never wanted anyone to see me as weak because everyone saw me as strong and having it all together. After all, when anyone had a problem they would come to me. They never knew I was battling with my own demons inside. I was losing it inside. I got tired of pretending and tired of hurting, to the point that I didn't care what anyone thought of me. I took the mask off and started telling bits of the things I was battling with inwardly.

I was hurting so bad that there were days that I would be angry with God and ask Him why I couldn't have a normal life.

Why did He let all this happen to me? Why did He let me endure so much pain? On sunny days, I would sadly sit in the house while my kids would be outside playing basketball, having fun with their friends. There were also days when I would walk around the corner from my father's house and sit on church steps and just cry my heart out. I would sit and cry while the events of me being molested played over and over in my mind. I tried very hard to see past my pain but I couldn't. I remember one day a nice-looking gentleman walked pass as I was sitting on the church steps. He stopped and said "Baby girl something is bothering you real bad because I can see it all over your face". He was right. I went to Pastors, family and friends and tried telling them what I was dealing with and they told me to "just pray about it". Some told me "you have to be strong", yet little did they know that I tried that for years and it never worked. The more I tried, the weaker I became.

Eventually, my children and I joined another church that I thought would make things better. It didn't, it got worse. The pastor of that church would get on the pulpit and rip the members apart. This pastor was mean and controlling, and when I noticed my mind started galloping like a horse. Something triggered from their controlling ways. It was like I was reliving the assault and I was in the bedroom again with my uncle when he molested me.

I was forced to do things I didn't want to do but this time it would be different. I wasn't about to be robbed of the little hope I had. And I still had a little hope because I was with my dad, the man who I *knew* loved me.

At this church, everyone was under a spell. The ladies couldn't wear pants, if they did they were told they were going to hell. They weren't allowed to go to movies or watch television. The Pastor would tell them the TV was the devil. On top of it all heavy tasks were laid on the congregation. They didn't have any time for anything because they were swamped with things to do at the church and if they didn't do them, they were considered disobedient. The Pastor would say "you can go to these jobs and work for these white people but why can't you work for God". They taught the parents to be hard on their children. However, they didn't have to teach me because I was already hard on mine; I didn't even allow them to leave the yard once we left church.

At the time, I had my two older boys do newspaper delivery with my father, because I wanted them to know the importance of working. They would complain to me about how tired they were because they had to be in the school an hour after they got done and then had to be in church early on Sunday's. Many Sunday's they fell asleep during service and were yelled at in front of the whole congregation.

They were told "get up in God's house, there isn't no sleeping in here". When I saw in their eyes how tired they were, I told my kids that they didn't have to deliver newspapers anymore. There was no way that I was about to make my boys feel the way I was feeling for years — like a prisoner.

My kids couldn't go over to their friends' house; instead, their friends were allowed over our house to play ball in our front drive way while I was on the porch making sure my boys didn't fall and scrape their knee. I was so afraid that if I let my children get out of my sight that they would get shot or something bad would happen to them, especially my daughter. I thought someone would do her the same way my uncle had done me. I was so paralyzed with fear.

Fear had a tight grip on me and I had a tight grip on my kids, so much so that I was choking the life out of them. I was choking their childhood out of them, choking out those fun precious moments that they only get to experience as a child.

My kids and I continued at this church and the more we attended the worse the teaching got but I stayed because I thought I was pleasing God by attending church. Sadly, all we ever heard about was an angry God that would get you if you messed up. We heard about a God that would get you and wouldn't bless you if you didn't pay your tithes.

We were in a cult. They taught that if you didn't pay your tithes, God would get it in another way. An example that they used that I always remembered was when the congregation was told that God would get His tithes even if he caused you to get in a bad car accident and you end up going to a doctor. You paying your doctor bill was proof that God got His tithe—this is what was preached. If you caught a flat tire, then God got your attention. Every time something bad happened in our life the pastor would say that is God whipping you, because He is trying to get your attention or you have been sinning. The Pastor taught that you couldn't be around your unsaved loved ones. The Pastor even preached about other Pastors and said they weren't saved.

Even though I attended this church I knew this wasn't God. And because I didn't agree with these teachings I was considered disobedient. I would cry out to God because I wanted to know Him personally for myself. I was tired of being abuses with religion in this church. I felt lost and the pain got worse. I knew this wasn't the message of God.

This is when the turning point started in my life, I started seeing the light at the end of my tunnel. And from that moment on I was called rebellious because I didn't follow their teaching. I left that church and attended another church that unfortunately taught the very same thing. But it didn't stop me from believing in God because I knew it wasn't the message of Christ. At this church it seemed like every time something bad had happened in our lives they used it as their Sunday morning sermon. We would leave church stressed and worn out each Sunday. My pain was getting worse and worse and it seemed like all hope was lost for me. I would be driving home after service hoping another car would run my car off the road and kill me. Again, my light at the end of my tunnel was getting dark. I felt like Martha the sister of Mary in bible (Luke 10:38-42). I was distracted by all the hard tasks from church and at home that I truly was missing out on a loving God and missing out on time spent with my children. It wasn't until I continued to cry out to God that I realized that the god that was preached about Sunday after Sunday wasn't the same God I was reading about in my Bible. As I prayed God would reveal to me what His Son Jesus done for me on the cross. The more He did the more I realize that God was a loving God and that He wasn't this angry, demanding God I heard about every Sunday. God revealed to me that His Son Jesus came down to earth, willingly, to take away all my past, present and future sins.

He showed me that he wasn't causing any of the bad things I was experiencing in my life because He sacrificed his Son for me on the cross. God revealed so much to me that my light at the end of tunnel had hope. After this, I still stayed in that church, hoping that the Pastor would see the truth about God when he opened his Bible. But he didn't because the devil kept a tight knot in the blind fold him had over this Pastor eye.

Despite this, things were great for my Sunday school class because I would teach about the good news of Jesus Christ. You could see the heavy burdens lifted off the members. The pastor and one of the deacons didn't like that this was happening. Every time I was in the middle of my message they would ring a bell, even though I would only be 15 minutes into the teaching.

They rung that bell like an annoying customer rings a bell at a checkout line. But it didn't stop the people from filling the church up Sunday after Sunday to come to my bible study class to hear the message of a loving God that gave up His Son for our sins. With the help of my sister Love, I started a program called Women of Destiny that I held every Tuesday. The program immediately took off. It kept growing and growing because the women were being set free from the devils lies.

When they left the program, they left with hope.

Although it was going well, eventually I left that church because I could no longer heart the message of condemnation being preached. And because I left, I had to stop the program because I had no place to hold our meetings. That Pastor was sucking the life out of me. I had to do what was best for my children and me. I had to be in a place where my children and I was getting fed spiritually so that we could grow in the knowledge of God because we were spiritually dead from all the false teachings we heard.

6

By that time my two oldest boys had enough so they started running away from home to hang out with their friends. Even though we were finally seeing the light, my children were already damaged from that false teaching and from the prison I held them in thinking I was protecting them. I would go and find them and bring them back but it didn't stop because they felt free by running away. They found friends that didn't judge them or beat them down like I did or like the churches did.

The reality was that their friends were dealing with some of the same things back home. It was a pack of them running away and at the time us mothers called these kids rebellious. However they weren't rebellious at all, they were hurting and tired. Like me, they wanted to be loved, uplift, encouraged and free so they ran hoping to find it in the streets.

When they started hanging out in the wrong areas and around wrong people I knew it was time for a change. So out of fear of my children getting gun down in these Decatur streets I decided to let them move back to Peoria, Illinois to live with my mother to finish high school, go to college, play basketball, football, and to stay out of trouble.

My son Tony was a great basketball player and my son Danny was a great football player. I really thought that my kids would do better in their home town especially because they wanted to move back to be with my mother and my family. I really had high hopes for them and I still do to this day. I truly thought in my heart I was doing the right thing.

Here I was trying to do everything in my power to protect my babies but I discovered it was too late. Little did I know my kids already started walking the path I was trying to escape. My kids were at the point I was at with God in the beginning of my life. They were angry with this mean God they heard about on Sundays and out of my mouth. At first, things were going great for my boys.

Then one day, as if all of a sudden, things took a change for the worse. Things went from bad to worse. My kids started hanging out with kids that came from the same background they came from. They came from fatherless homes, dysfunctional homes, abusive homes and religious homes where negativity was being crammed down their throats. My boys started smoking marijuana because they thought it would help them cope with the pain they were dealing with inside and because they wanted to smoke it because they thought it there was nothing wrong with what they were doing.

My kid's life at the point had spiraled out of control but I never lost faith in God. What I realized I actually destroyed my kids when I thought I was doing the right thing by protecting them. I realize I had did the very thing my uncle had done to me; I took my kids choices and when I did I cause them to rebel. Just like when my uncle took away my choice to be a virgin. When he took my choice I gave up all hope to live because I was always under the assumption that my life would always be destroyed. I never knew I could live past the pain my uncle caused me. Here my kids were dealing with the same issues I tried to keep them from dealing with. They were on the same path I was finally walking off.

I was finally overcoming my nightmare but my kids were just experiencing it. For me I found myself right back on that road with my kids when things changed into a very bad nightmare when I got the worse phone call of my life that turned my whole world upside down.

7

In the midnight hour on August 12, 2012 the telephone rang shocking me out of my sleep. You should have seen the frantic look on my face as I jumped up out of my sleep. I looked like I was in a scary Halloween movie; the look on my face was like the lady with the heels on running from Freddie Krueger. I was scared. I knew something had to happen for someone to be calling me in the middle of the night.

"Hello?" I answered with a scared tone in my voice.

"Demetria," my mom responded on the other line. "The police are here looking for Tony."

"For what mom?" I asked confused as I was rubbing my forehead?

"Well, Demetria, they would like to speak to you".

"Ok, put them on the phone."

"Hello Demetria, I am from the Peoria Police Department and I am looking for your son Tony Harris". Immediately my heart dropped. I just knew somebody had killed one of my babies. Beside all I ever heard growing up is if the police ever calls you late at night it is because somebody has got killed. Well I found out that isn't always true.

"Officer is my son alright or did he hurt anyone?" I frantically asked, anxious to find out what was going on.

"No, your son is not hurt and no he didn't hurt anyone. But we believe that he shot at one of our officers and we are out looking for him. Do you happen to know where he's at?"

"No sir, I am in Decatur." My heart was pounding in my feet. I am surprised it didn't wake my dad because it was pounding so loud—at least that's how it felt. Not knowing what to do, I got down on my knees to pray. As I was praying fear was staring down at me like a giant ready to eat me up like prey. But that night me and fear stood toe to toe because I wasn't about to let fear paralyze me and keep me from praying. I wasn't about to let fear make me think that suicide was the only way to deal with this. I knew God could handle anything so I took my weak tail right to God in prayer because he said in his word that his strength is made perfect in my weakness.

I needed all His strength that night and I mean *all of it*. I said in prayer "God I truly don't know what's going on and Lord I hope this is all a dream. God, can you touch my son's Tony's heart and have him to call me because Lord I don't know where my baby is."

That moment it felt like someone snatched my heart out of the bottom of my feet where it fell because I couldn't even get up and stand to get back in my bed. It felt like I was losing my breath. *This can't be real.* As I whispered those words it felt as if God's strength was flowing through helping me stand and get back in bed. I sat on my bed rubbing my head.

Ring, Ring.

"Hello, who's calling?" I said answering the phone.

"Mom, the police are trying to say that I shot at one of their officers." Tony, said in a frantic tone.

"Did you son?"

"No mom". We stayed on the phone a little while longer talking like a mother and son would. I ended our conversation with prayer and by saying "Tony, I am going to call my sister Kay and see if she would take you to the police station in the morning to turn you in because you have to turn yourself in."

I eventually went to sleep but it wasn't easy because my mind was crammed with all types of thoughts.

I fought through those thoughts like a heavy weight champion because I meditated on God's promises. One particular, one God said that he will never leave me nor forsake me. I knew I wasn't alone and I knew that God would see me through whatever was coming behind this.

That next morning, I got up bright and early to call my sister to see if she would take my son to turn him in. I called her before I brush my teeth and before I washed my face.

Ring, Ring.

"Kay, this is your sister Demetria, can you do me a favor?"

"Yes, what it is."

"Can you meet Tony down on the south end to take him to turn himself in because the police have a warrant out for his arrest"

"For what?" They said he shot at one of their officer."

"What for real?"

"Yes and I need you to go with him to talk on my behalf."

Sunday morning my emotions were everywhere as I was getting dress to go to church to teach my Sunday school class. My emotions were all over my bedroom, I couldn't even see how good I was looking in my mirror on my wall. As I was getting dressed my phone rung and on the other end of the phone line was my sister Kay. She said that when she went to meet Tony he wasn't there.

I stopped everything I was doing to catch my breath because I felt myself passing out. I thought this had to be a nightmare. What is going is what I asked myself over and over again. I told my sister thanks for being willingly to take Tony, as I hung up my end of the line. I sat there in disbelief because I was hoping my dad would come in my room and wake me up from this nightmare but he never did because it was reality. I had to realize this is not a nightmare.

After I got done praying I got up and headed to church because at the time I was teaching my Sunday school class. That particular morning I was teaching about God's love and right in the middle of my teaching. I stopped and told everyone "how can I teach you guys about God's love and not teach my son about it?" I told them that I am done with class today because I am about to go to Peoria and turn my son in.

I didn't know how I was going to get there but at the time I didn't care how I was getting there. If I had to walk I was going to get there. I then proceeded by asking my dad could he take me. His response was nothing I wanted to hear so I called my younger sister Nisha and asked her if she could come and take me to Peoria.

Prison Mom

She said yes. "As a matter of fact I am in Bloomington about 30 minutes from Peoria be ready" is what she told me. I rushed home and pack my children and my bags because we lived right around the corner from the church. I felt so disconnected from everything. It was like I was in a big empty world by myself with pain. All type of thoughts ran through my head but I kept meditating on God's word and that's what gave me hope in such a dark time to hold on and not give up.

8

As I arrived in Peoria the police were everywhere searching for my son. It was like the national guards had paid a visit to Peoria to apprehend my son. That's how many there were. It was so many of them that I thought my son had killed a police. They were watching my mom and other family member's house while looking for my son. They had their house surrounded like ants do when they find a piece of bread on the ground. So, I had my sister to drop me off at the police station because I didn't want to have Tony to meet me at one of their houses. I didn't want them to have to deal with the cops searching their homes. They were already dealing with enough from the stares of the officer who were sitting out by their house watching their every move like they were the ones they were looking for. I called my son Tony and told him to meet me down there at the police station.

When I finally arrived to the station I stood there waiting, the sun was scorching my dark chocolate skin. You would've thought I was in a sauna room in a sauna suit sweating off pounds the way that sweat rolled down my face to my feet. The wait seemed long. I felt like I was in a dark fog but in that fog I started singing amazing grace. While singing, I noticed a burgundy car pull up in the parking lot of the police station.

However, I only saw one head which was one of Tony relatives who drove the car to dropped my son off at the police station. I walked across the street to ask her where was Tony. She said in the trunk of her car. I was so shocked and sadden to see my son crawl up out of this trunk as I opened the trunk of his cousin car to get him out. I grabbed my son and held him tight. I never knew that day would be the last day of seeing my son. I truly thought that this would all blow over. I remember telling my son that if you never trusted God then this is the time to. I said son this is not the ending but it's a new beginning as I whispered in his right ear. I held him so tight because I didn't want to let him go. I even held my tears back because I didn't want my son to see me cry.

There I was standing in the front lobby of the police station trying to play strong but I was weak. I was so weak that I'm surprise I wasn't arrested from disturbing the peace because my knees were loud from knocking together from shaking.

Eventually I let my son neck go and walked to the clerk desk holding my son hand. I told the clerk who we were and our reason for being there. Before I knew it about 4 police officer came running out from the back.

They ran so fast that they literally almost ran us over with the bottom of their tennis shoes. They immediately placed my son in handcuffs and took him to a room in back and close the door behind him as he sat down at a little old wooden table with two old chairs that look like they were falling apart.

They left me standing on the other side of the door with them even though I thought that second chair in the room my son was in was for me. But as we stood on the outside of that room in the hallway, they told me that I had to wait out front.

"Officer My son is only seventeen and by law I am supposed to be present with him". I told him.

"Mam, your son is being charged as an adult" one of the Officers said.

"What are you serious, what happen to gathering your evidence first," I snapped. A person is innocent until proven guilty. They had already had him charged with attempt murder to a police officer. What I didn't understand at that moment was how in the hell can they charge him with a crime that was never committed.

An officer was never shot, hurt or harm. From my understanding the only way a person can ever be charged with attempt murder is when he or she has shot a person above the waist that indicates that he or she has attempted to kill his or her victim. However, here I was standing between two or three officer trying to teach them the law that they supposedly have learned in police academy school. I was so furious that I walked from the back in slow motion because I couldn't believe what I just heard. As I stepped into the lobby Tony's grandma and his aunt on his father side was sitting out there waiting to see what was going to happen. They were sitting there looking so sad and scared.

As for me and the look on my face, you couldn't tell if I was coming or going because my face had the strangest look on it. I still to this haven't discovered the look I wore on my face that day. I truly don't believe that look exists. I sat down and started praying asking God to help us and strengthen us. I was weak and in shock. I couldn't believe what was going on. Before I could say amen to end my prayer an officer came out and said "Mrs. Williams, we are charging your son Tony Harris with attempted murder of a police officer. We will be escorting him by patty wagon to the Peoria County Jail."

They weren't even back there five minutes so where did they get their junk chargers from I asked myself. I then asked him can I meet you in back where you're taking my son so I can see his face. I wanted to see if my son was still the way I brought him in. I also wanted to see if they were pulling a joke on me. I also wanted to see my son off. The officer said yes! So I ran out of the front door of the police station to the back to see my son while Tony's grandma and aunt went to get the car they drove in to pick me up from back to take me back to my mother's house.

When I got back there the officer said "sorry but your son is already in the police wagon". I stood there in disbelief because I couldn't believe how fast they got him out of the station into the transport wagon because it didn't take me two seconds to get back there. I ran back there like the world greatest track star. I eventually ended up getting in the car with Tony's relatives and as we were leaving out of the parking lot I noticed the police wagon pulling out of the garage of the police station so I asked the driver did he have a Tony Harris in his wagon. He looked at me and stuck up his middle finger. This really upset Tony's family. I told them that was the devil not that officer. As Tony's aunt was driving back to my mom house to drop me off. I was stuck in a trance. Things didn't seem real. Here I was trying to figure out what happen. Was this really happening? Is my son really going to jail?

When we pulled up at my mom's house a few of my family members was crying and some was very angry with me for turning my son in. They couldn't believe as a mother why I would turn my own son in. They said some of the harsh things about God because I told them that I was going to trust in God know matter how bad things looked, even though my heart was full of pain. My heart was used to this though, pain wasn't new to my heart. As a matter of fact my heart and pain became the best of friends behind my fleshly body.

I realized that moment I had no choice with pain and my heart becoming the best of buddies. I ended up having a disagreement with one of my siblings because she was very sure that the police was going to take my son somewhere and beat him before they took him to the county jail. She yelled this with a frantic voice, I realize now that she was just scared. I told her that God was with my son and that he's not going to allow it.

I said God is protecting him. We went back and forth with a loud commotion. We were so loud that we were disturbing the neighbors. We also had the attention of friends who was at my mother's house and the neighbor's attention. It didn't cool down and the loud commotion didn't stop until my mom's house phone rang.

My mom answers it and accepted the call from the Peoria County Jail. Tony was on the other line. She asked Tony was he alright. He said yes. She asked did the police touch him. His response was no. She yelled "he said the police didn't touch him!" Everyone looked at me with a shock. As they looked at me I felt betrayed by my family. It seems like when I needed them the most they weren't there. They looked at me like I had did something wrong to them. I got on the phone with my son and we talked and ended our call with a prayer. I stayed at my mom house on her porch because I couldn't face anyone because they had my son picture on just about every media outlet. And just about everyone in Peoria knew about my son arrest. I didn't feel like talking to know one at the time because I was still trying to process all of this and I sure didn't want to be judge as a bad parent. I ended up staying in Peoria for about a week. During my stay I visited my son Tony at the Peoria County jail. We had a great conversation about trusting in God. At the time I didn't know how I was going to pay for a lawyer, I didn't have a clue because I wasn't even making minimum wages. I didn't know what to do. But I kept praying to God because one thing I did know is that God was with me because He promised to never leave me nor forsake me. I knew that it wasn't God punishing my child. I also knew that God didn't cause this to try to get my son attention or my attention. I knew that God had punished His Son Jesus Christ for our sins

2000 years ago (Romans 3:21-31). I held on to God's promises like never before. Well eventually weeks later of trying to sale hot cooked meals to scrap up money to pay for a lawyer my mother and one of my sisters agreed to pay the lawyer fees. They hire a lawyer out of Chicago Illinois who was good at winning all of his cases. He was great that the Peoria Courthouse system hated him for great line of work as a lawyer. At that time my son's case was a high profile case that most lawyers in Peoria wouldn't take. My family and I believe the reason for that is because they felt like the city of Peoria would look at them as a trader or because one lawyer informed us that if they won the case for Tony then their family would have been harassed by the Peoria Police department for the rest of their life.

9

While sitting in a waiting room with my mom and three of my sisters at the hospital visiting a relative the news came on the television in the waiting room where everyone was sitting. On the news was a picture of my son and his chargers. People in the waiting room were talking about it. They said things like that's a crying shame what that kid has done, they were saying so many bad things.

One man, and his wife was sitting next to my family and I, and he was talking about it. As he was talking he overheard me talking to my mom and sisters. I was telling them that I am going to trust God. I told them I know it seems like things are out of control but I knew that God was in control.

The gentleman proceeded by saying "Miss, I am so sorry to hear about this but I love your spirit. I will be praying for you and your son." I told him thanks because I needed all the prayers I could get because things were dark for my children and I. My other children were very sad. I didn't know what to tell them at the time. I watch my other two boys suffer in pain and disbelief. My kid's hearts became best friends with pain just like mine was.

After things had settled down, I finally returned to Decatur where I was staying with my father. The concerned phone calls stop and the rumors started. I was called a bad parent, my son was called all sorts of bad things, and we were the topic of everyone's conversation. The rumors were so bad but I took it all to God when I was praying because I couldn't bare all these lies on my weak shoulder. Time went on not allowing me time to gather my thoughts, but thank God for his patience because he let me gather my thoughts. He made sure that I was conscious of his word at the time instead of the devil lies that was being placed in my mind.

The devil had bombarded my mind with his lies. He said things like you are all alone, you should gone commit suicide because your life will always be full of pain, you will never experience joy or peace, he also said you are curse, look at all the bad that has happened in your life.

I thank God that even though the devil lies was roaming around in my mind I didn't mediate on them because I knew from my past where the mind goes the body will follow. I knew if I would have sat there and meditate on the devil lies I would of believe him when he said commit suicide and the rest of his lies but I didn't because I was meditating on God's word. His word kept reminding me that I was never alone because God promised to never leave nor forsake me.

As time went on I noticed that my third son grades started rapidly changing. They were going from A's to F's. He even stopped playing basketball even though that was something he loved doing. Every time I tried to talk to him about what was going on he would try to avoid the conversation. He wouldn't open up to me instead he suppressed all his feelings yet it kept seeping out in his behavior. He was so angry. I remember one day I heard him singing "God please give me my brother back." I responded saying God didn't take him. As I was talking to him I noticed that he had markings all over his arms with his brother name. I watched my son as he was drowning in pain. My son was experiencing that very thing I tried to protect him and his siblings from — pain.

Prison Mom

I realized at that moment I had failed at my attempt to keep them from that dark road I traveled on. I noticed that he had started smoking marijuana to try and escape the pain he was dealing with inside. It was so hard for me as a mother watching my son come home with his eyes blood shot red from smoking marijuana. I tried talking to him, I tried punishing him, and I prayed with him hoping he would stop, but he didn't. He just got worse. It felt as if he was taking everything out on me as if I had arrested Tony and sent him to jail.

At that time in our lives, I wore my knees out from my wooden bedroom floor. I didn't skip a beat from praying. During those times while I was praying, God revealed to me that my son was angry with him and he revealed to me that my son was using marijuana to cope with the pain he was dealing with inside. God was revealing to me how he was going to show me how to be gentle and patient with my son. While I dealt with him on one hand, I had my other children on the other. My daughter would cry to me and just seeing her tears would make me cry.

My oldest son seemed like he lost all hope because he lost not just a brother but a best friend. He and Tony were inseparable. Anyone would have sworn they were identical twins. They had so much in common that no one understood, not even me.

They both lost their father to death; they both grew up with the teaching about an angry God; they both grew up in the house with a hurting angry mother and the list goes on and on. I realized my trauma and Tony's conviction didn't just turn my world upside down, it also turned my children worlds upside down. Our lives were rearranged. But my faith was the same. I never doubted God because I knew he was with me through it all.

10

For about a year and a half I was driving back and forth from Decatur to Peoria for court. I was missing work and my younger two children were missing days out of school just so I could be at all of Tony's court dates. This was the longest year of my life. Every time we went to court they would continue it. Going back and forth wore me out. I wanted this to all be over because I got tired of seeing my son shackled down from his hands to feet in chains and handcuffs. I hated seeing him like that. During those times I wanted to kick into mommy mold and rescue my son. I wanted so badly to take my son home with me. I just wanted to put on my super mom cape that superman had given me to use his powers to snatch Tony up out of the courtroom and fly away, but I couldn't.

I was hoping this was all just some type of nightmare. There were days I wished his father was alive to deal with this. To be honest, I even convince myself that maybe his father knew this day was going to come so that's why he left this earth. Yet I knew it was the pain that had me thinking this way. I had to realize his dad was murdered; someone took his life, keeping him from being here with his son. It was difficult but we pushed through, after a long period of time the trial finally begun.

My family and I met at the courthouse to be in court with Tony. One day Tony's lawyer pulled me to the side in a room at the courthouse so he could discuss Tony's case with me. During our conversation, he made a past at me. This man had undressed me with his eyes. I felt so uncomfortable but at the time I overlooked his lustful eyes because I wanted him to win my son case. I told my family what he did and one of my relatives said "If I was you I would sleep with him to get my son out." I couldn't believe what I was hearing; I had to check my ears to see if some wax was clogged up in there. It wasn't, I was hearing correctly. I responded saying if my sons freedom is based on me having sex with his lawyer then he will never be free because I won't be doing that. I finished by assuring them that I would continue to trust God.

A month after that while I was at home on my computer God placed on my heart that Tony's lawyer would stop representing him. That same day Tony's lawyer said that he was going to be at the courthouse for another client. Since we owed a balance, I asked my sister Love if she could stop by the courthouse to pay him.

Since she was in Peoria she went to the courthouse to pay him 1500 dollars of his lawyer fees. To her surprise he wasn't there. Love called me to inform me of his absence so I called him to see what had happened. He said his case was rescheduled so that's why he wasn't in Peoria. I proceeded to tell him that my sister came to pay him some of his money. When I told him the amount he said that he was done representing him. "I wanted $3,000 because that's what me and one of your relatives discussed" he told me. Before I could even respond, he hung up the phone. I sat there at my computer stunned, like *WOW God*; you *just* revealed to me that Tony's lawyer will no longer be representing him and here it is happening.

Weeks after that, I went to Peoria and while at my mom's house with my mom, aunt and a few of my siblings the phone rang. It was Tony calling collect from the Peoria County Jail. I accepted the call and my son and I started talking about how much we love and missed one another. He then asked how everything was going.

"Son, you no longer has a lawyer to represent you." I sadly informed him.

"What mom, are you serious?" he yelled.

"Yes, son, I'm serious" I said and went on explaining to him what happened.

"Mom, I need a lawyer. These people are going to try and hang me."

"Son, I am going to trust God because I know that he has already worked it out."

"I am tired of you talking about this God s**t!, that's all you talk about every time something happen" one of my siblings said going on and on ranting.

"Now you are wrong don't do her like that" my mom responded defending me. I told my mom it was alright because in my heart I knew he was just scared and hurt about the whole situation, after everyone left out to go outside. I pulled him aside and said "I want you to know that I forgive you because that wasn't you. That was the devil. He's the one that's tired of me trusting God. He was hoping that this would cause me to lose my mind."

After a long time of praying, trusting God, and searching for lawyers my mom and family got another lawyer to represent Tony. He was a lawyer out of Peoria. Finding him helped to finally speed everything up, we were finally at the moment I was waiting for—the trial. I was waiting for this all to be over and I was hoping for the best through it all.

The morning of the trial I woke up praying. As I was praying God placed in my heart to get my family and pray with them. He said *Tony's life is in my hands. If they offer him life today let your family know that I am in control.* As I left my mom's house to go to court, I met up with my relatives and some of Tony's friends outside of the courtroom. We went deep—there were so many of us that you would have thought we were at a wedding reception. I said to each of them that were standing out there "let's pray because God is in control." When I prayed, I prayed a special prayer for my niece because she and Tony were real close. I prayed for God to give her strength that day. She hadn't made it down to the courthouse yet because she was running late. After we got done praying the ballot opened the door to the room so that we all could come in the courtroom where they were holding Tony's trial at. Slowly, we all walked in one by one.

Everyone looked nervous. The jury was sitting there like they had hope in their hands waiting for me. The judge on the other hand, was sitting at his desk rubbing his short black silky hair. Tony's' lawyer was sitting across from the state defense team and my smiley face Tony was sitting there in awe, happy to see all the support he had.

Tony's lawyer did his final argument to the jury to convince them why his client shouldn't be found guilty.

I thought he did his thing. After he finished, the young lady that was representing the state did her final argument stating why Tony should be found guilty. She said that he should be locked away for the rest of his life. She tore my sons' character apart, painting him as a monster to the jury. For the life of me, I couldn't see how they could charge him with attempted murder when the officer was alive sitting in the courthouse. He was never shot and had no old wounds that could prove it and a gun was never found in my sons' possession. After the closing arguments, the Judge talked to the jury members and informed them of their role—they were to go back in the room to deliberate whether or not my son was guilty or not guilty. Once he did that court was dismissed until the jury came with a final agreement.

Everyone left the courthouse and Tony's lawyer said that he would call us when the Judge instructed him to. This was the longest wait ever. Every time the phone rang, I answered it immediately. After hours of waiting we finally went back to the courthouse. When we entered the courtroom, everything seemed different.

There were detectives and officers standing inside with their hands on their guns. I knew right then and there something wasn't right. To my horror, I was correct.

My son was found guilty and charged with attempted murder of a police officer. When the judge read the verdict, my family burst into tears. However, my niece I prayed for didn't; she said "Aunt, I feel your spirit. It's at peace because you know God is in control." I responded saying "Tt, I am at peace with trusting God." I knew that moment if I never trust God, *that* day was the day to trust Him. Yet, even though I was trusting God my heart was still aching.

The Judge gave my son 55 years imprisonment. After announcing the sentences, he asked Tony if there was anything he had to say. My son responded saying "yes". He stood up and thanked his lawyer and told the Judge, God bless him. I then stood up and thanked the Judge and Tony's lawyer for everything. I asked the Judge if I could hug my son. He refused saying "No Mam', I can't let you do that."

What stood out to me that day, and still to this day, is that a gun was never found in my son's possession. The officer was never shot. In fact the offices simply said that he *believed* he was shot at. There were never any shell casing found at the scene of the crime or anywhere in the area the cop was in. Despite this, I am trusting God because I know for a fact something good is going to come out of this. No, I don't understand what's going on. And no, I don't like what's going on.

What I do know is that God is not surprised about what my son is going through. As a matter of fact, God *already* knew what my son was going to go through before He formed him in my womb. I also know that God is not punishing my son because God punished His Son, Jesus on the cross for our sins. No, God didn't send my son to jail to get his attention or my attention because God doesn't force anyone to accept His Son Jesus as their Savior. He lets them freely choose. I knew all of this, and I believed it even then; yet the pain that came with that sentence was pain like no other. That day it felt like someone snatched my heart out of my chest when the officer walked my son off to transport him back to the Peoria County jail.

11

As my sister and I were driving back to my mom's house from the courthouse, we talked about the case. She thought what happened was unfair and I felt the same. I told her "Sis, God is in control. He will work it out for out good," When we arrived at my mom's house, my mom was sitting there waiting for us—she was so nervous. She didn't go to court because she couldn't take it. She looked at me and asked me if I was alright. I said yes. She asked me how I do it. I responding saying it's nobody but God because if it wasn't for his strength during my weakness, I would have lost it all; I would have checked out a long time ago.

What they didn't understand was that I didn't know why I wasn't able to cry. I asked myself these questions because I didn't understand why I was able to go on during this devastating time. What I knew was that there was no way possible in my own strength I could have made it through something like that. I knew it was God and no one but Him. He held me up and gave me strength to make it through that day. However not everyone saw it that way. "I am going to be dead when Tony gets out!" My mom said devastated by the news. I assured her that she wouldn't and that she would still be alive.

That day I received all type of phone calls from just about everyone that knew Tony and I. They were calling to see how I was doing; however, all I wanted was for my mom to hug me and hold me in her arms. That day I needed my mother's touch. I felt like a little helpless puppy left alone in the midst of growling wolves. After some time, I eventually returned back to Decatur because I had to be back to work. The phone calls stopped and everyone went back to their normal lives. When checking in stopped, the gossip started.

Family and friends started talking about my son and I blaming me for the situation. I was portrayed as a *bad parent*. I dealt with so much from family and friends.

Some family members would mock me and say things like "*My* kids know better. I taught *my* kids to get an education" and so on. As if I didn't teach my son the same thing. They would boast in my face on how good their kids were, and although I wanted to, I never said a mumbling word. I just took it all in because I knew it wasn't them. I knew it was the devil trying to make me feel like a worthless mother and make me believe that my son was a monster.

I didn't hold it against my family. The more they said bad things. the more I prayed for them. Things went on like this forever with people and their harsh opinions about me and my child.

I dealt with so much from society. It was easy for people to judge but what everyone didn't understand was that it was hard for me seeing my son in this predicament.

Yet, I never confronted anyone. Instead, I kept praying and trusting God. It hurt to hear those horrible things being said about me from friends and family. Especially because, this was a time I needed them the most yet they turned their backs on me. For the first couple of years I would pray to God asking Him to not let me take it personal with my family. I asked God to help me to continue to love them and He did just that.

Even though I continued to love them, I felt like my family forgot all about my son because they were no longer writing him. His friends also stopped writing him and even stopped asking about him. Apart from one of my sisters and one of my friends, it was like my son was dead to everyone. It hurt me to the core to see everyone that proclaimed they loved my son, vanished. In spite of this, I took all my hurt to God and asked Him to help me forgive them.

12

After some time, Tony was finally transported to Pontiac Correctional Center. I decided to go visit him because I just wanted to hug him. I wanted to be able to hug him so tight and never let him go. I took my daughter and my sister along with me. When we made it to the prison I had to show proof that my daughter was my child and provide identification for myself; my sister had to do the same. As the man was putting all our information in the computer, he noticed that there was a stop on my name from Decatur Women's Prison that said I couldn't visit anyone in prison. I said

"What? are you serious sir?" I exclaimed not fully understanding what was happening.

"Yes Demetria, I am serious" he responded.

"What is that?" I asked confused and frustrated while on the verge of tears.

"You must go and talk to the Warden in Decatur, to get that off your name. Because it's there, I can't let you visit your son today. I'm sorry."

I was so hurt. My daughter and I held one another while we cried. Our tears dripped all over that prison floor. She told me that she would hug Tony for me and tell him how much I love him. I told her ok and left out of the prison while her and my sister went to the back to go visit my son.

I left out of there with so much pain in my heart. I just wanted to see my son and hug him because I hadn't seen him in months. I got back in my rental car and drove to an empty parking lot and just cried out to God. *God what's going on? I know you got to have a plan behind all of this.* It seemed like the more I trusted God the more the devil was throwing darts at me. But by God's grace I kept going because I knew no matter how bad things looked and felt, God was working it out for the good.

At 3pm that afternoon I went back to the prison to pick up my sister and my daughter. As they were coming out from the prison, there was a big smile across their face. That moment I knew the visit went great. They got in the car and told me how much my son said he loved me and how he missed me.

"Sis," my sister said turning to me. "God is really holding your son up. The way he was talking, you wouldn't believe he was in jail because he got so much hope in knowing that God is in control and that He is working it out for his good." I was so happy to hear the good news but I would've loved to just hug my son. That's all I wanted to do. I just needed a hug.

***

About 2-3 years later, as I was getting ready for work early in the morning I got a free phone call from the Peoria County Jail. On the other end of the phone was my oldest son Danny, telling me that he was in jail.

"*Jail*, For what son?" I asked shocked as to what he just told me.

"Residential burglary" he answered and then the phone call ended. I couldn't believe what I just heard. *Not again.* I couldn't believe this was happening and it took me a while to get myself together. I finally left the house and arrived at work. I went into the building of my job and did my regular work duties acting as if nothing happened. It wasn't that I was trying to hide it and it wasn't because I was ashamed. I did this because I couldn't believe this was happen all over again.

I remember standing at the cash register feeling like I was in a dark fog. However, I never stopped trusting God because I knew He was with me because He promised to never leave me nor forsake me.

At 11am that morning I went on my 15-minute break. While on my break I got my phone, and went on Facebook. The first thing I saw when I got on Facebook was a post on my niece page. It said:

Ya'll wrong for leaving my cousin Danny like ya'll did. Ya'll know that wasn't his stuff he got caught with. Danny would never have all that stuff.

I commented on her post asking what was going on because honestly I didn't know what she was talking about. I was blind to everything. She showed me the Peoria daily commitment report. It read that my son was charged with drugs and guns. "What?" I said to myself confused. This couldn't be true because my son never sold drugs and he never owned a gun. Needing to clarify I called my niece to see if she had more information and to find out who else was involved in this situation. "Danny didn't do that by his self. That's just not Danny, aunt" she assured me. We talked some more before hanging up. I went back on my nieces' page on Facebook to read all the comments people put under her status. Every comment I read pretty much all said the same exact thing my niece said—this was not Danny's character.

When my break was over I went back to the cash register to continue working. As I was working, I was in my mind praying asking God to reveal to me what was going on because I was in a state of shock. I asked Him to continue to strengthen me because I felt so weak.

Later in the day, when I got off work, I called home to Peoria. My family confirmed what I saw on Facebook, telling me that my son Danny was charged with drugs and guns. Yet, my son never sold drugs or owned a gun.

I couldn't believe it. I was trying to process everything, because I couldn't believe I was going through this all over again. What made it worse was the rumor circulating around. The rumor was that one of my relatives put my son Danny up to doing this. So many rumors began to circulate and so much confusion was happening that I didn't know what to do or say. To put an end to it all, I called the Peoria County Jail to see what my son was being charged with. Just as my family said, Danny was charged with possession of guns and drugs.

13

I kept going to work and going on about my everyday life while pain was invading my heart. Yet and still, I was trusting God through it all. Some people asked me how I could go on after all I went through. I told them God was the reason I was able to make it through. I knew for a fact if I didn't have a personal relationship with God during this time, I would've lost my mind. I also knew if I was under that religion teaching I was previously in, I would've checked out because that teaching teaches about an angry God. A teaching that God causes bad things to happen in your life to get your attention; that he is an angry God that is sitting in heaven waiting to punish you for everything you do wrong.

I thank God that I am no longer under that false teaching but I am in a personal relationship with a loving God, who punished His Son for me, my child and every person on this earth. I knew I was in right standing with God because Jesus Christ made it possible for me through his death and resurrection. I also knew that God loved me and my children and I knew God *wasn't* the cause of this.

This started from a dysfunctional home. Another reason I was able to go on is because I had already been through it with my son Tony. No, I am not saying that I loved what my children and I was going through what I am saying is that during these dark times of my life, God was my light.

Eventually my son Danny was sentenced to seventeen years in prison. From the moment my boys were incarcerated, so-call family members and friends talked behind my back. I was called a bad mother and I was even considered cursed by some of these people. Despite this, I truly thank God during these times for being my strength and for carrying me on. Some people thought I was pretending when I would respond saying "I am wonderful" every time I was asked how I was doing.

These people couldn't understand how I could be doing wonderful after all I was going through. Some people ridiculed me right to my face. As if I was the worse person on earth and my kids were monsters. I remember many days feeling compassion for these very people.

They didn't know that their kids weren't exempt from the things in this world; yet, somewhere in their little bitty minds they thought they were a better parent than me because their kids weren't in prison. In their eyes, they were the perfect parent. However, during all of this I never lost hope in God's word.

I knew God was with me. I knew He had a greater purpose for all this bad. I knew that He knew all that my children and I was going to go through before He formed me in my mother's womb and before He formed them in my womb. I knew God wasn't sitting in heaven surprised by my boy's incarceration. As a matter of fact, He knew before it even happened; He had the expiration date. God has always been in control and always will be.

14

The hardest things I have dealt with since my boys' incarceration is their father's being deceased. It has been many days I wished that they were alive to help deal with things because on this dark road I just wanted to sit down and take a break. I wanted to run and hide out on a secluded island. There were days I just wanted to hear "Demetria, take a break and just relax. I got this for you." The most difficult times are during the holidays and my boy's birthday's because I miss my boys being home with us. I miss celebrating their birthdays with them. But of these, the hardest thing I have struggled with and still do as a mother, is going to the prison to visit my boys, because when I leave I can't bring my boys home with me.

On two of my visits with my son Danny I have cried my heart out both when I hugged him and when I left. He held me so tight, trying to console me and said "Mom, don't cry." What he didn't understand is that he was my baby and always will be.

I cried because I never dreamed of my kids going through something like this. I also cried because I knew when I left the prison he couldn't leave with me. Even through the tears, one thing I never did was lose hope in knowing that God had a great plan behind all of this.

I remember one time when I took my younger children to visit Danny, my youngest song Elijah made me cry. When it was time to leave Elijah said "I am not leaving mom, I am staying here with my brother." I told him that he couldn't and that he had to leave with me. "Elijah responded saying "No mom, I don't want to leave my brother." That tore my little heart to pieces. I was speechless. I had no words to give my hurting son and it hurt. I never knew how bad leaving would affect him after his visit to see his brother. Once I finally got him to leave, he walked behind me with tears running down his face. It hurt me to look back and see my son crying.

We eventually got in my car to drive back to Peoria to visit my mom. As I was driving tears began rolling down my face when I looked in the rearview mirror and saw my daughters' face drenched in tears.

"Please stop crying because ya'll got me crying" I said to them not knowing what else to say.

"Mom, I don't ever want to go back there" Elijah blurted out through his tears. It was at that moment I knew my son was hurt that he couldn't stay with his brother or because his brother couldn't leave with him. To see my kids hurting, pained me in ways I can't even explain. After a few moments of silence, I finally mustered up words.

"Son, I don't understand this situation at all but I do understand God is with us and that He does have a great plan behind this all. One day we will all reunite as a family again no matter how bad things look."

Having two siblings in prison has affected my babies in ways I never imagined. I watched my son Elijah drift away in his pain. He started hanging around the wrong crowd. He just didn't care about life anymore because he lost two of the closest people in his life. I remember praying to God daily about Elijah because I refused to sit back and ignore my sons' sufferance. So, I did what I knew best and went to my knees.

"Dear God , give me all of Elijah's' pain. I can deal with it God because I have dealt with pain all my life. God I know you are a pain killer. I know you are with us. I know you have a plan but right now God my son Elijah is blaming you for all of this…" On different occasions I would hear my son pleading with and begging God to please let his brothers go and also see him writing those exact words with ink on his arm. I knew my son didn't understand what I understood. So, I prayed to God daily on my son behalf.

My daughter on the other hand would cry when she talked about her brothers but I really don't think she fully could understand the concept of what was really happening. Yes, she missed them much and she would do anything to have them home with her but I truly don't think she was affected the way Elijah was.

Another difficulty we all faced was not being able to see Tony. When I first started writing this book, it had been two years since I last saw Tony. I believe one of the reasons is because I knew how difficult it was going to be to leave him behind after the visit and how difficult it was going to be for my two younger siblings. Yet I couldn't take it anymore. I missed him. And after two years I finally built up the courage to go see my son. I didn't care if I cried; I just needed to hug my baby.

When we arrived, I finally got past the lady and man in the uniform sitting behind a glass window putting all my children and my information in a computer. I was so fearful that day that they were going to say I couldn't see my son, so I left out the information of my experiences in jail in my younger days.

I knew I was taking a risk, but that day I *had* to see my son because I desperately *needed* a hug from him. I hadn't seen him in two years. I started crying the moment they sat me and my two younger kids at the visiting room table so we could wait for Tony to come out. My two younger children tried their hardest to hold back their tears but they didn't have any luck. They couldn't hold back those forceful tears. Those tears demanded their way down my children face.

Yet, just before the officer brought Tony out all of our tears disappeared, they vanished from off the earth of our face and somehow, out of nowhere a smile appeared. One by one we took our time hugging Tony. I held him so tight that I didn't want to let go. We played the game Uno together and we ate good. There is a machine in the prison where you can buy a card and load it with money. I loaded it with a bunch of twenties that way we could eat as much as we wanted. I wanted to make sure my son Tony was really full because I knew he was tired of eating that slop they were serving him every day.

While we were there, Tony and Elijah had an awesome talk.

"Elijah make sure you always listen to mom because I don't ever want you to experience this. I wouldn't wish this experience on my worst enemy," Tony said. Tony made sure he drilled that information in his little brother's skull. Eventually our time was up and we had to leave. Out of know where, tears came pouring out of all of us, except Tony. Tony on the other hand wore that big bright smile he always wore from the moment he came out of my womb.

No matter what he was going through, he faced everything with that pricey smile that sat on his handsome face. This time things weren't so bad for Elijah as they were when he visited Danny.

Yes, he cried and yes, he wanted to stay but he didn't cry on the way riding home. Instead, he laid in the back seat of the car with his headset on his ears and drifted away into la la land.

Weeks later I got one of the most difficult and frustrating phone call from my son Tony. He informed me that I could no longer come and visit him or his brother because I didn't put all my past offensives on the paper I signed. I couldn't believe what I was hearing, I was sick and tired of being treated like I was a criminal. Yes, I committed some crimes in my past but I paid my dues to society. I am a mother, a pastor, an author and I work hard.

I changed my life all the way around, but it didn't seem like it because I was paying for my crimes over and over again. Although I knew God had cleaned my slate, every time I went to visit my son Tony, my slate was following me like a stalker follows a person. I was *very* upset. The only way I could ever get to see my kids were through a visit at a prison: not at a soccer game, a basketball game or even at parents teacher conference. The only way I would see my sons were at a hard iron table at a prison for only a few hours. Yet here they were trying to take my *only* few hours away. I eventually got a letter in the mail from Menard Correctional Center where Tony was housed stating that I was permanently taken off the visit list from seeing my kids. "Over my dead body," I said to myself as I read the letter.

This has been one hell of a ride but guess what I am going to ride this ride until the rodeo falls off. I refuse to lose my few hours. I apologized for not putting *all* my information on the app but what I don't understand is why for the life of me I am being punished. As a mother, all I want to do is see my son and hug him because I don't get this chance every day. I only get this chance every other month or every other year and only for a few hours. I need this visit because seeing my children's' face, helps me to go on.

Unless a person has a child in prison it can be difficult to understand all the frustrations that come with it. Another issue I had to overcome is dealing with the anger towards my boys and the anger that comes with struggling to keep money on their books. I recall times I would walk into a Kroger store to use their Western Union System, being mad with my boys for being incarcerated. I would say to myself "I wouldn't have to put money on ya'll books if ya'll was out."

My daughter would look at me like I was crazy as if I had lost my mind. To be completely transparent, I was very angry with them for being in prison; but I thank God for helping me to overcome that anger because I realized being angry wasn't going to change anything but my attitude.

There were times that I struggled keeping money on their books because I just didn't have it and because nobody was helping me. I had one very special person who did her best to help me and she did an awesome job but it was still hard because I was trying to stretch my $8.75/hr. I was making at my job. I truly thought I could do what Jesus did with the three fish and five loaves of bread. Here I was trusting in my own ability instead of God's strength. I also was struggling because I had a problem with being a good steward over the money God was giving me through my job.

I was unfaithful steward because I ran to a store every time I got paid to make sure my daughter and son had the new Jordan's that came out every week or to buy clothes for them. They didn't need them because my closets looked like they belonged to a hoarder. I also was spending money on myself. I had no control over how I spent my money.

My kids and I didn't need all the things I was buying, yet I kept buying. The money had power over me. It wasn't until I started praying and asking God to help me be a good steward over my $8.75 that I started to see a change.

I was damaging my kids with material things. No, I am not saying it is a sin to have nice things because it's not. But raising your child up on material things will destroy them. It's important to teach them that their value is not in things but it is in Christ.

It doesn't make you a bad person if you're not buying your child every pair of Jordan—it makes you a wise person. It doesn't make sense to see Michael Jordan's bank account over flowing while yours is struggling to keep the five dollar balance fee so your account won't have overdraft fees. It took me years to learn this vital information and guess what, I am *still* learning. The difference is I am no longer struggling to keep up with people who are struggling like I was. I am free because of Jesus Christ. Now I am able to send my boys money.

It hasn't been easy because I never dreamed in a million years one of my bills would be a prison bill but I have learned the most valuable lesson—I was struggling because I was doing things my way instead of God's way and because I was depending on my own self efforts instead of God to provide for my children and I. God has taken my $8.75 and did what he did with the three fish and five loaves of bread, because it has been feeding a multitude including my children and I. Because of that, I am no longer struggling. I depend on God to provide for my incarcerated children, my other two children and myself because after all he says in his Word "Don't take no thought for yourself." He's letting me know that I need to stop trying to see how I am going to provide for us because it's his responsibility to do it.

15

Before I go on, I want to slow down a tad bit and explain something very important. I know many of you are asking plenty questions: "How can you be so sure that God is with you?"; "How can a good God let bad things happen in your life like this Demetria?"; "How are you so sure that God has a plan in all this bad?"; "Do you feel cursed?"; "How can you have peace in the midst of all the chaos you have been through in your life?" Well I am here to tell you, I am glad these questions are asked because I get to share about God and His wonderful works. I will be sharing some wonderful stories from the Bible that can relate to my life.

One thing I know for a fact is that God promised me in His Word that He would never leave me nor forsake me. I believe His promise because I know He is not a liar. I know He always speaks truth because after all I have been through, He has been the reason I never lost my mind. I know that at some time in life, every person has been hit with a storm in the form of situations, circumstances, obstacles, problems, and difficulties. And during those times it seems like that storm is going to overtake you. I have been hit repeatedly with storms after storms.

These storms hit me to take me off the course of God. They have tried to deter me and keep me from being all God wants me to be, from having all God wants me to have, and from doing all He wants me to do. These hits are from the devil. He was hoping his hits would take me out, but thanks to God for being a great anchor. I know for a fact that I have a great foundation and that foundation is Christ Jesus. In fact, He says in His Word, in John 16:33, "you have tribulation and trials and distress and frustration." It is so important for me to understand this so I won't be confused and lose my faith in Him when life is hard. Jesus tells me in His word to be of "good cheer" because He already overcame everything in this world for me. I know it seems like I never get to see the rainbow after the storm or a sunny day.

I want you to know that the Son is always with me in every storm I have been hit with, that's why I am still standing and going on. That's why I know God is with me every step I take.

I also know what happens when I lose faith in Christ in the midst of a storm. I sink with worry, fear, and discouragement. I learned to not focus on my storms because when I do they will take over. Instead I focus on Christ.

I recall what happened to Peter when he took His eyes off Christ and started looking at his storm when Christ told him to walk on the water. Matthew 14:28-33 "And Peter answered him and said, 'Lord, if it be thou, bid me come unto thee on the water.' And he said, 'Come'. When Peter came out of the ship, he walked on the water to go to Jesus. But when he saw the wind boisterous, he was afraid and began to sink. He cried saying, 'Lord, save me.' And immediately Jesus stretched forth his hand and caught him, O thou of little faith, wherefore didst thou doubt? And when they came into the ship, the wind ceased. Then they that were in the ship came and worshipped him, saying, of a truth thou art the Son of God." Peter and some disciples were in a bad storm in the mist of the sea. It was being tossed with heavy waves. And Jesus went walking to them on the water.

They were fearful so that's why Peter asked if that's you Lord bid me to come to you on the water.

When Peter started walking on the water he focused on the storm and how big it was getting. And when he did that he sunk. But the moment he called Jesus' name he made it safely through the terrible storm. Just like Peter, when we focus on our problems instead of Christ we sink because we lose faith in Christ and the idea that He is bigger than anything life throws at us. I want my readers to keep in mind that bad things happen every day, all day, in this life we live in. These are attacks and assaults from the devil to distract us from the perfect good will of God but we can overcome through God when bad appears in our life. Not by our own strength because our strength is fragile. It is too weak to deal with the cares of this world that's why God tells us to cast our cares on Him (because he cares for you) and "He shall sustain them: and He shall never suffer the righteous to be moved by the bad things that appear in his or her life" (Psalms 55:22.) God is letting us know that we can make it during the worst of times. If you make up in your mind to go against the devil by trusting in God when something bad appears in your life, you will encounter some opposition and persecution for trusting God. The devil wants you to feel like God is cursing you so that you can take your trust out of God. He wants you to believe that God has left you and forgotten you. But do not become discouraged. God has a word for you, "Fear not, for I am with you; be not dismayed, for I am your God. I will strengthen you, yes I will help you, I will uphold you with my righteous hand" (Isaiah 41:10). In the life of Jesus as well in the life of Paul, people didn't exactly stand up and cheer because they were healing sick and casting out devils. As a matter of fact, some people were happy but others were greatly disturbed by these miracles. Stephen was stoned to death and James was beheaded. Paul was persecuted constantly, not for doing wrong but for doing well. In the Bible every person that had their trust completely in Christ and not in their own self efforts or another human being went through so much during their life time. As you can see the devil only attacks people who are a threat to him and his kingdom.

For example, anyone that knows what Jesus Christ has done for them on the cross. He attacks those people because he doesn't want them to spread the good news of Jesus Christ.

When you are not a threat to the devil, he doesn't give a care about you and what you are doing. I want you to remember that bad things have happen to others and that God is for you, remember, God is going to help you. The devil wants you to believe when bad things happen in your life that God is punishing you. He is trying to get your attention and tell you that you are cursed by God. But I served him notice that he is a liar. I want you to always keep in mind that God's Son, Jesus Christ willingly came down to earth to take your punishment and every curse that was against you.

In John 10:10 in the Amplified Bible Jesus said, "I came that (you) may have and enjoy life, and have it in abundance (to the full, till it overflows)." God is our Helper, our strength, the One who will lift us up. Romans 8:31 says, "If God is for us, who can be against us?" Think of this: *If God is for you, who can prevail against you?* Joseph's brothers were against him, but they didn't prevail over him.

Daniel had all the governors and leaders against him but they didn't prevail over him. Paul and Silas had officials who were in position of authority come against them but they couldn't prevail over them. It is important that we get this word inside of us: *if God is for us, no one can prevail against us.* No weapons formed against you shall prosper when you trust in God. Yes, the weapons (trouble) will come but they will not cause you to have a nervous breakdown, stress, worry, be depressed, fearful when you are relying on Christ and His supernatural strength.

Romans 8:28 says, "And we know that all things work together for the good of those who love God, who are called according to His purpose." When you place your faith in God's Son, Jesus Christ, then you can say, all things are working together for good in my life. Even if you haven't placed your faith in God's Son yet, things are still somehow working out for your good but you will not be able to see that good unless you are in Christ.

If you are living for Jesus, then you took a stand against the devil and he doesn't like it.

He is against you and he will try anything to destroy you. This means you will encounter him head on. But I want you to keep in mind that Jesus defeated him on Calvary. The devil will throw all types of hits at you hoping to make you feel like you are defeated.

He tried it with Jesus, Paul, me and he will try it with you. Wherever Paul preached and ministered, he was opposed. Jesus from His very first message was criticized and ridiculed. In His first hometown sermon, they tried to throw him off a cliff and kill him. That was just the beginning of the opposition He encountered during His teaching and sharing. Everywhere He went, Jesus faced storms, criticism, slander, and wrong words spoken about Him. People lied on Him, laughed at Him and rejected Him. If Jesus overcame all these storms, then you can overcome all the bad things you receive in life because He lives in you.

Yes, your storm may be different from mine but I want you to know that through Christ you can make it during a storm and you can overcome any storm. Whether the storm is the loss of a child or loved one, or if it is sickness or disease that tries to rob you of your physical health, or a loss of a job or it can be a financial storm.

It can be a storm of worry and anxiety that tries to come against the situation you are faced with. It doesn't matter what the storm is, *you will make it*. I know for a fact you can make it through any storm. I am not telling you something I heard, and I am not writing something just to make you feel good. I am telling from my own personal experiences that you will make it through any storm when you have faith in Jesus Christ because his strength is perfect.

16

Another reason why I trust God and His word is because He showed me in a dream things concerning my boys that are incarcerated just like He showed Joseph. From a young age Joseph believed God had destined him for greatness. In dreams God assured Joseph that he would rise to a position of leadership over his parents and brothers (Gen. 37:5-11). My dream was different from Joseph. Mine was my two older boys in a house fire.

The house was a very nice big yellow house. This house was on fire with my two boys in it. I stood outside with all my family, friends and other people I didn't know, surrounded by three fire trucks and a load of police cars. I stood there in faith while everyone else was yelling and crying because the house burnt all the way down to the ground. The only thing was left from this fire was ashes and rubbish. In the dream the fire department said no one could survive through this. It looked like it was over and that my boys were dead.

But in this dream my boys came running out to me when everyone thought it was over for them. They weren't burned and they didn't smell like smoke. This is how their situation looks to everyone.

It looks like it is over for my boys. It looks hopeless but I stand in faith knowing that it is not over for my boys and that there is still hope for them. I know that God has a great plan for them out of this bad situation. Our situation is a fire and it look like we will not recover from this because it looks like this will destroy us. It won't because God is with us. We will not look like what we going through. Thanks to Jesus Christ!

Recover

I want to give you specific insight and strategies to help you make it when your world is turned upside down, so that you are empowered with joy, peace, and endurance. First, I would like to acknowledge that I am weak and that the reason I am strong is because of God. It's His strength that's keeping me strong during my weakest moments. I want you to know that if I wasn't relying on God for His super natural strength then I wouldn't be strong. I would've lost my mind.

Second, I cry just like you cry but in my crying, I keep faith in knowing that God has already worked this situation out for my good. I don't care how bad things look, God is in control. In the next couple pages, I am going to give you some tools that work perfectly during difficult times. These are 5 tools that I have used and still use for overcoming the storms that appear in my life.

Toolbox

Tool #1
Keep your mind on God's promises
Isaiah 26:3

"You will keep him in perfect peace, whose mind is stayed on You, because he trusts in You." Now if we look for lasting peace elsewhere, we won't find it. If we think anything or anyone in this world can give us peace when we are faced with a storm then we are fooling ourselves, only God. Only God will Isaiah 26:3. Not maybe, not probably, not shoulda, woulda, coulda — *He will.* In the midst of storms, mediate on God's Word by spending time reading it because where the mind goes the body will follow. If we don't mediate on God's Word then our mind becomes idle.

The Word says "an idle mind is the devil workshop" (Philippians 4:8). The person who meditates on God's Word of the Lord is like a tree planted by rivers of water, Alive, thriving, strong, and mighty. We need to take our thoughts captive and replace them with the Word of God. After all our thoughts are not our thoughts.

They are the devil lies he placed in our mind because our mind is his battlefield. He uses it to place hopeless thoughts and every type of bad thought in it. Because he knows if he can control our mind then our body will automatically follow. We need to condition our minds to respond to adversity in a Godly manner rather than dive into self-pity, cursing, rage and impatience. "Do not be conformed to this world but be transformed by the renewal of your mind, that by testing you may discern what is the will of God, what is good and acceptable and perfect." How do we do this? By Philippians 4:8. Meditate on those things. Meditate on God and His Word, His handiwork and majesty.

The devil will try to plant thoughts in your mind. For example: "God is punishing me every time something bad appears in life. God doesn't love me that's why all this bad is happening in my life. God can't be with me during this situation I am facing because I feel all alone." Phrases such as this proves how subtle the thoughts are the devil plants and if you allow your mind to, it will run wild and meditate on every thought the devil plants there. Instead, when we choose to meditate on God's promises our mind is kept in perfect peace by God.

Before I continue, please keep in mind that renewing our mind doesn't happen once and for all then the devil will leave us alone. In fact it is an ongoing process. We should make up our mind to meditate on God's word every time the devil tries to fill our minds with lies. It is then we can become victorious every time. I recommend that we meditate, reflecting on God's word *every day*; not just when trouble appears in our life. This way, when trouble does come we can stand against it instead of being shaken.

What I do each morning when I awake and before I start my day is I ask God in prayer to help me to be conscious of His promises and my identity in Him, because I understand that every day the devil tries to plant lies in my mind. However, because God's word is also being planted in my mind the devil has a struggle because my mind is not idle. Instead is occupied with God's word and His promises. And guess what keeps my mind peaceful? When I am conscious that God is with me and that He will never leave me.

I am conscious that He loves me unconditionally and there's nothing I can ever do to stop Him from loving me. His love is not based on me or my merits but it's based on who God is. He is love. I am the righteous because of Jesus Christ obedience on the cross and not by right doing. Jesus made me right with God when He paid the price for my sins.

You see, it's when you know that your righteousness is from the Lord and not your own doing will you be victorious in your mind against the devil lies. It shows him that you are at rest in God.

Rest indicates that you are not worrying, reasoning in your mind, anxious, or letting your mind run wild. You have come to the understanding that God said you never seen the righteous forsaken or his seed begging bread. This rest is God's peace that's in your mind. When your mind is resting then your body is stable.

I want you to understand one last thing about me and my life. My life didn't change when I started church. My life didn't completely change until I changed my way of thinking. It changed when I started replacing the devil lies with God's truth. The thing is the devil doesn't care about you sitting in church faithfully every Sunday or during every bible study. What He does mind you doing is replacing his lies with God's truth because he knows if you do so, he has no control over your body.

In the beginning of my book, you read about how bad my life was after my mom and dad separated and after I got molested. I believed wrong and because of that I lived wrong. But when I started replacing the devil lies with God's truth I started living right.

I became victorious. I was able to rejoice during my storms because I knew that God wasn't the cause of my storms. I knew God was with me and that He was working the bad out for my good. I knew God had a perfect plan in every storm I faced. I knew that God loved me with a never-ending love. I knew God wasn't punishing me because I knew that He punished His Son on my behalf. I knew that I was His beloved who He was well pleased with because of His Son Jesus Christ and not because of something I did. But it was by faith in His Son Jesus Christ that He was pleased with me. God moved by faith and faith alone. It is impossible to please God without faith. Hebrew 11:6 "And without faith, it is impossible to please God, because anyone who comes to Him must believe that He exists and that He rewards those who earnestly seek Him. When it comes right down to how God interacts with humanity we see that our faith is the leading substance that invites Him and maintains His presence into our lives. Moreover, faith is also the substance that cuts through the physical realm and connects us with God in such a powerful way. Faith in God is the basic element that enables us to acknowledge and revere His absolute existence and divine presence. This lead us to grasp the fact that the supernatural realm into which God dwells is far more real and powerful than the natural one into which we live. Faith is also an indispensable necessity in order to please God. We will never be able to fully comprehend as to why faith is such a critical matter to the extent people own eternity hinges on whether or not they're willing to exercise faith in God on the basic of Christ's finished work on the cross. Faith starts off with acknowledging the absolute existence of God, which pertains to His invisible qualities, His eternal power and divine nature in the creation of the world (Romans 1:20). And the belief that He's a rewarder of those who earnestly seek Him, which then relates to whom God is (Exodus 3:14, Philippians 4:19, Proverbs 16:3, Jeremiah 29:11, Numbers 23:19). In short, faith is built upon these two colossal pillars which are knowing that God exists. Our faith in God through Christ is the core foundation upon which our lives as Christians are built. Faith is what makes Him becomes real into our lives. Whenever we allow unbelief to get the most of us, we literally turn God off. Unbelief is a poison for both unsaved people's eternity as well as our relationship with God, and having a firm belief that He rewards those who earnestly seek Him.

Faith is not the absent of storms but it's having complete trust, confidence and assurance in God right in the mist of any storm. Faith knows that God has already worked it out even though you can't see it right now.

Even though you don't "feel like it" but you can't let feelings deter because they are fickle. Faith is trusting God completely and that comes by asking God to help you trust Him completely. I want you to know before I wrap this tool up that the devil will harass our mind all the days while we're here on earth. But I want you to know when we choose to believe right we are victorious and the devil is a defeated foe. Artist Brandy once said "It's really about changing your mind and your thoughts, replacing negative thoughts with positive ones.

When you practice positive thinking enough, the picture of your life starts to look different. That's just the way life works; it happens in your mind first." I back her up one hundred percent. Joyce Myers also knew this because she wrote one of the greatest books called *Battlefield of the Mind.* Please start watching what you are thinking! The key to living victorious is replacing the devil lies with the truth of Christ Jesus. Not just sitting in a church full of people. You must know and apply the gospel of Jesus Christ in order to live victorious. He came to set the captive free. Not bond you with religion, rules, tradition, laws, or legalism.

Christ wants you to have a personal relationship with Him by faith and not through your self-efforts. If it was possible that you could please God through your self-efforts than there was no reason for Christ to come.

He came because it's through having faith in Him that we please God, faith in knowing that He paid the price for your past, present and future sins. Faith in knowing that by His obedience you are made righteous the moment you receive Him as your Savior because He gives you the gift of righteous. It's not by your right doing are you made right with God but it's by having faith in Christ that you are accounted righteous, Romans 4:2-6, "For if Abraham were justified by works, he hath whereof to glory; but not before God. For what saith the scripture? Abraham believed God, and it was counted unto him for righteousness. Now to him that worketh is the not reckoned of grace, but of debt. But to him that worketh not, but believeth on Him that justifieth the ungodly, his faith is counted for righteousness. Even David also describeth the blessedness of the man/woman, unto whom God imputeth righteousness without works."

We are not counted righteousness by what we do. Attending church doesn't make us right with God; singing in the choir doesn't make us right with God; paying our tithes doesn't make us right with God; feeding the hungry doesn't make us right with God. The only thing that makes us right with God is Jesus. That's why Abraham was counted righteousness by belief. I want you to know that the moment you make Jesus your Savior, you are right with God. Jesus gave you the right to be righteousness. *It is gift!*

You see, you can never boast about anything because you haven't done anything right that made you right with God. All it takes is faith! I am living proof that you can make it through any storm when you got faith in Jesus Christ. Faith does not mean trusting God to stop the storm but trusting Him to strengthen us as we walk through the storm.

Tool #2
The tongue has power of life and death
Proverbs 18:21

What are you saying in the midst of a storm? Are you listening to the words that are coming out of your mouth? We must understand what we say will infect us in ways we can never imagine. I know in the midst of storms we can say the most hurtful things. Because we are fearful, hurting, discouraged, and angry with God because some of us think that He's causing the storms. That's why God tells in His word that death and life is in the power of our tongue.

Like I stated in the first tool it is very important to believe right because when we do, we live right. God wants us to be a person whose mouth is full of life. But our mind must be full of life first. If my mind is full of death then the word that comes out of my mouth will be death. The words you speak will depend on what's filling your heart. So, fill your heart with grace by soaking in the bible.

Be very careful taking in the words of death in the newspaper, radio, the TV, face book, or the blog.

Instead pray: "Set a guard , O Lord over my mouth; keep watch over the door of my lips!" (Psalm 141:3). If you are speaking words like, "I am going to lose my mind behind this; this is going to be the death of me; this is going to cause me to have a heart attack; there's no way I can recover from this. You're just like your no good father; you're a failure; you're a disappointment to the family, or etc...." you are speaking words of death out of your mouth. These type of words show that you have no hope. And when we use these words we cause our situation to die. A lot is in stake in what we say today. Especially when we are faced with a storm. Yes, I know that it is hard to say words of life in the midst of a storm. But I know that it can become easy when our heart and mind is full of life. *How can we fill our mind and heart with words of life?* By reading the Word of God and meditating on His promises I wrote about in tool 1. When we do that, we speak words of life out of our mouth because out of mouth flows rivers of living water. This living water is God's word. His word says, I will never leave you nor forsake you, this bad is working out for my good. He said be of good cheer during trials and tribulation because "I already overcame everything you are facing." God's word fill us with the hope of knowing that we can make it through Christ during a storm. So, while we're in a storm we can speak words like, "I don't understand what's going on and I don't even like what's going on but I know I am not alone in this because

God is with me. I know God is working this out for my good. I know God is not punishing me because He punished His Son on my behalf. I know He has a great purpose for this thing the devil meant for my harm. I know I will not lose my mind because God promise to keep my mind in perfect peace. No I want have a heart attack. As a matter of fact, I am victorious because of the strength of the Lord that's keeping me strong during my weakest time."

A self-righteous tongue will say things like "God is punishing me because I didn't go to church. He's trying to get my attention by causing me storms. God is punishing me because I didn't pay my tithes. You're being punished because something you did wrong, because you don't go the church more than the next person." That self-righteous tongue will say you're facing this storm because you're curse—just like Job friends did him. They came with words of death instead of life when Job had lost his children, business and everything else. Instead of them comforting him, they made him feel like he had did something wrong so God was punishing him.

So many people react to crisis and tragedy by asking, "Why me?", blaming God for their pain and even turning away from the Lord. Yet in the midst of all his suffering and his friends discouraging words Job continued to acknowledge his dependence on God. Job had no idea why all this was happening to him, but he continued to trust God. Notice Job did not charge God with wrong. The big question that people have asked through the years is why does God allow bad things to happen, and like Job we do not always know the answer to that question because God didn't promise us an explanation but, He did promise to never leave us nor forsake us. We may not always understand why, but there are some things of which the bible assures us; "For I consider that the suffering of this present time are not worthy to be compared with the glory which shall be revealed in us. And we know that all things work together for good" (Romans8:18,28). Thus, we can be assured that God does have a plan whether we recognize it or not. With this attitude we can use the storms of life and trust God and let Him use them for our good. Be like Job, don't let the self-righteous friends of yours cause you to ever think that you are going through storms because God is punishing you or trying to get your attention. Self-righteous people think that the reason things like this is not happening in their life is because they're doing something right with God or because they're bless and you're not but they miss out on the whole point just like Job friends did. Job's self-righteous friends accuse him of some terrible evil to deserve what he got. God allowed the devil to test Job because the devil said the only reason why Job trusts you is because of everything he has. I bet if you take it all from him, he will stop trusting you. God spoke highly of Job. "He said have you considered my faithful servant Job? You can take all he got and he still going to trust me." The devil really thought by causing storm after storm in Job life that Job would stop trusting God. He thought Job would make a shame of God by blaming God for the storms but the devils plan backfire. Job did the opposite. He trusted God.

In my case with my two boys going to prison I knew it was from wrong beliefs that cause them to be in prison. I know God didn't send them there to get my attention or to punish them. What the devil meant for my harm God is using it for my good. He thought my children incarceration would cause me to lose my mind. He thought that I would blame God for it. He thought I would turn away from God and stop trusting Him but I thank God for His supernatural strength that's keeping me during this storm and during any other storm I face.

Just like the book of Job is God's inspired answer to the issue of suffering in life, my story is to inspired as well.

Again, in this life we may never fully understand all the whys and wherefores, but there are some conclusions that we can reach based upon what God has revealed in His word. Whatever happen God is still there, He is still in control, and He always cares for us (1Peter 5:7). He may not necessarily remove the storms that we face, as in the case of Paul's thorn in the flesh (2Cor.12:8-10). However, He will bless us to have joy in the midst of our storms, to trust Him and to continue to say He is good in the mist of bad. He will bless us to speak life during our storm instead words of death. Also, be careful who you allow to comfort you when you are faced with a storm. If that person words are not hope filled from God then that person will speak death into your ears and you must keep in mind whatever you let go through your ear gates will eventually come out of your mouth. For example, if a person sits around every day at work on his or her lunch break and listening to music with negative lyrics, listen to bad news on television every night or sit around negative people daily, then they will begin to speak negativity because all the negative words have entered into their ears. You must surround yourself around people who speak life during your storms. That's why it's important that you spend time reading God's Word so that you are feeding your mind because the devil is going to make it his business to try and plant his lies in your mind. People die because of something said. Tongues can be weapons of mass destruction, launching holocausts and wars. Tongues can also be the death of marriages, families, friendships, churches, careers, hopes, understanding, reputations, missionary efforts, and governments. But people also live because of something said. The tongue can be "a tree of life" (proverbs 15:4). Tongues reconcile people and make peace. Blessed are the peacemakers (Matthew 5:9). Tongues can make marriages sweet and healthy, families strong, and churches healthy. Tongues can give hope to the despairing, advance understanding, and spread the gospel. This can only happen when a person's mind is occupied with the words of God. When a person's mind is filled with words of hope, peace, and joy then out of that person mouths will come words of hope, peace, and joy. *What will come out of your mouth today, death or life?* Swords thrusts or healing? (Proverbs 12:18) It will all depend on what's filling your heart. Jesus said, "Out of the abundance of the heart (the) mouth speaks" (Luke 6:45). A critical heart produces a critical tongue. A self- righteous heart produces a judgmental tongue. A bitter heart produce an acerbic tongue. An ungrateful heart produces a grumbling tongue. A person mind that's conscious of God's word and not the devil lies produces a hopeful tongue. That's always filled with joy and peace because once a person mind is renewed by the word of God then that persons heart is filled with the word of God. Again, where the mind goes the body follow. Because a loving heart produces a gracious tongue. A faithful heart produces a truthful tongue. A peaceful heart produces a reconciling tongue. A trusting heart produce and encouraging tongue. That's why it is so important to fill your heart with God's grace by soaking in your Bible. In the midst of a storm or and every day period be a person whose mouth is full of life. "And now I commend you to God and to the word of His grace, which is able to build you up "(Acts 20:32). You can have peace in the mist of your storms by speaking life or you can have discouragement in the mist of your storm by speaking words of death It is your choice. Remember whatever words you choose to speak have the authority to empower God's blessings or Satan's curses in your life.

Tool #3
Worship
John 4:23-24

Worship confuses the devil because he's expecting the storms that he created in our life to destroy us. Worship is a life response to the worthiness of its object. When we worship God, we do so in response to who He is (Psalm 52:9). Our attitudes and actions reflect that we believe the character and conduct of God to be worthy of praise and adoration. God is a spiritual being. And He tells us in His word to worship Him in spirit and truth. Why is that? Because our spirits is the core of who we are. It is the center of our volition and our emotions.

So, to worship in spirit then is to do something that is beyond the physical. We do not worship by bowing our knees but we worship through the heart (Psalm 51:17). Our worship is in line with the worship that's in heaven (Psalm 148:1-2, Ephesians 6:12, Revelation 4:8). Now worship in truth is that we worship based on the truth about who God is and what God does. Why He is worthy of worship. It also includes the truth about our circumstances.

We worship God in the mist our of storm, heartache, loss or whatever we are facing. When we worship Him, we don't forget about, but we worship Him in the truth of our hurt. No, we are not worshipping Him for the hurt, the storm, the heartache or loss but we worship Him for His goodness, His strength that keeps us when we're weak, the peace of mind He gives us for keeping our mind on Him in the storm, for His faith He gave us to believe that He is working the bad out for our good, for His joy, for His majesty and must of because of who He is. He is God and He is bigger than anything we face. And there's nothing too hard or complicated for Him. Now to worship God in spirit in truth is to declare that He is worthy of our reverence no matter what's our circumstances. When we do this, we are showing the devil that no matter what happens in my life God is with me because He promises to never leave me nor forsake me. We are letting that devil know that God is not the one to blame for my storm but He is. We worship God based on the truth of who He is, the truth of who we are. The truth of what God does. No, we don't worship God for our hurt because if the truth be told none of us like pain but we worship Him because what He is going to do with our hurt. He said that what the devil meant for our harm, He will use it for our good. We worship Him because He is just worthy. No matter what we go through in this life God will keep us during it and He will see us through the other side.

When we worship God we enter His presence and our mind is off our situation. For example, Paul and Silas two disciples of God was beaten so badly and thrown in prison. One day they were going to a place of prayer. On the way they saw a female slave. Someone who had a spirit that helped her tell what was going to happen in people's future. She made so much money this way for her bosses. She was a fortune teller. That day she followed Paul and Silas around shouting these men serve the most high God. They're telling people how to be saved. She followed them for days shouting this. It finally made Paul upset so he spoke to the spirit in the name of Jesus Christ. He commanded it to come out of the girl. And it did (Acts 16:16-18). The girl bosses were so mad because they were using this slave girl as a fortune teller. People were paying her money to tell them what was going to happen in their lives. Keep in mind as you're reading that the devil started out as an angel in the beginning but he was proud and wanted to be like God so that's why the evil spirit in the girl shouted that Paul and Silas was from the Most High and wanted to save people. That was the reason why the devil and many of the angels was thrown out of heaven because they sinned against God. So, you see they have always known the truth that God is the everlasting, all powerful God. But they didn't want to follow God. They choose to follow their own way. The girl bosses were so mad with Paul and Silas because all their funds had stopped that very moment they cast that spirit out of the girl. They didn't want her to be free because that meant they would be broke. They could no longer benefit off her condition. They couldn't take advantage of the poor girl any longer. They cared more about the money she was making for them then the girl. They were so mad that they beat Paul and Silas because they said they were causing trouble. They were thrown in jail after they were beaten and ordered by the jailer keeper to keep a close watch on them. The jailer then put Paul and Silas in a cell in the center of the prison. They chained their feet and all. The jailer did everything he could to make sure they were shackled down because he knew if they got away he was in big trouble. Paul and Silas were punished for doing a good thing. But the bosses lied on them because they couldn't benefit off that girl any longer. I am about to share with you how God had it all under control. God took this terrible storm and made it into something so wonderful (Isaiah 61:3).

Around about 12:00 midnight Paul and Silas were praying. They were singing songs to God. The other prisoners were all listening to them because they couldn't understand how could these man be singing during something so bad (Acts 16:25). We know that prison is not a place where someone is happy to be. Prison is often noisy.

Prisoners may complain about the food, or scream to be set free. Guards often yell at the prisoners and treat them wrong. These prisoners never heard anything like this before. In the pitch dark and in the middle of the night Paul and Silas sang praises to the Lord. This was unusual. A sound that caught the attention of every other person in the prison., Even the jail keeper. They notice something different about these two prisoners. Because the way they praised God in the middle of their trouble. You may wonder how as well. You may be thinking how could they sing at a time like this? You're probably asking how they can worship God for being beaten and thrown in prison. You're probably asking didn't they see their wounds from being beating? Didn't they know they were unfairly chained up in a prison cell? Paul and Silas praised God because they were filled with faith and with the Holy Spirit (Acts 11:24). Faith is being sure of what we hope for. It is being certain of what we do not see. (Hebrews 11:1). Paul and Silas were sure that God had not forgotten them. They knew God was with them. And that He would never leave them nor forsake them. They knew God wasn't punishing them. They knew the devil caused this bad but they was certain that God was going to work it out for their good. They knew God had a great plan even though it looked like an ending for them. Paul them was filled with Holy Spirit. One of the fruits of the Holy Spirit is joy (Galatians). You notice I didn't say happiness. Joy is different from happiness. Happiness is based on your circumstances. If things are going good you are happy. If you get a gift from someone you're happy. Happiness comes when something is going good around you but it disappears when things are going bad. Joy on the other hand when things are right in the inside. And only God can make things right for you in the inside. It is inner gladness and peace you have because you believe in Jesus. Joy doesn't change when our circumstances change. Joy is deep down inside of us. I know you heard in your life "this joy that I have the world didn't give it to me and the world can't take it from me." This indicates that joy comes from the Lord and it indicates that joy doesn't change when my circumstances change." Because of their joy given by the Holy Spirit Paul and Silas worship the Lord. Anybody can praise God when things are going good because things are going good around them but only a few can praise Him when things are going bad because things are right on the inside. We should praise God in good times and in bad (James5:13). Praising God is proclaiming His greatness because His greatness never changes, even when our circumstances changes. When you are face with a storm, when you are in a difficult situation, when you lose a love one and when you don't feel like praising God. But that will be the perfect time to make the devil mad. When we praise God during tough times, it invites God's power into our lives (Psalm 50:23, 2 Chronicles 20). As they were praising God, a powerful shaking came that shook the prison inside out. It shook it so hard that it blew the prison doors open and every prisoner chains were broken and came loose. It caused the jailer to wake up. As he woke up he saw the prison doors open. He pulled out his sword to kill his self because he thought the prisoners had escaped. Paul shouted with a loud voice don't kill yourself. We are all here. This made the jailer fearful. He fell to his knees shaking in front of Paul and Silas. He asked them what he must do to be saved. They told him to believe in the Lord Jesus. And then you and your family will be saved. Then they told him and his family the plan of Salvation. They accepted Christ into their heart as their Savior, as you can see what happen when Paul and Silas was praising God. God shook the earth on their behalf of those he wanted to save. The chains fell off the prisoners. Paul and Silas could have easily escaped. But this how we know that they were led by the Holy Spirit. They didn't run because they knew God had a great purpose in the beginning. They could have seeked revenge but they were filled with the love of God. They didn't take things personal with the jailer instead they knew the jailer was blinded by the devil lies. The Holy Spirit let them know that God did not cause this powerful shaking in the earth to set them free but it was caused to set the jailer free. As you can see Paul and Silas were inside the prison but the prison wasn't inside them. However, the prison was inside the jailer. He was bound up by the devil from his mind down to the depth of his soul. The jailer was chained up spiritually. Paul and Silas were chained up physically. I want you to understand one thing. Worshipping God is not saying that we love our storms and we are happy about what we are going through. It is simply saying that we reverence God for His deity and because of the joy of the Holy Spirit inside of us. Demetria what if I don't believe in God? Sweetheart, I will tell you that it is impossible to have joy in the midst of a storm.

As I stated early in this chapter that joy comes from God and God alone. I want you to know that you don't have to be in church to receive this joy but you must receive God's Son Jesus Christ as your Lord and Savior to receive this joy. I want you to know that Paul and Silas weren't in a church singing, they were singing in the darkest place, prison but they were in Christ. And that's where their joy came from.

As a result the other people in that dark place heard them praising God. They heard the truth about the mighty, living God. And it caused so many people to accept Christ as their Savior. Anyone can complain. Only those who are filled with the power of God can give thanks and praise when times are difficult, when you do this in the darkest times.

You will shine like a bright star in darkest time. Others will be able to see that and be drawn to God. Your praise invites God's power into every situation. Paul wrote, do everything without finding fault (complaining) or arguing. Then you will be pure and without blame. You will be children of God without fault in a sinful and evil world. Among the people of the world you shine like stars in the heavens. You shine as you hold out to them the word of life. (Philippians 2:14-16). I have a question: How do you act during a storm or unfair situation? Do people hear you complain like everybody else? Or do they hear you praying to God and praising God?

Tool #4
Pray
Proverbs 3:6
In all thy ways acknowledge him, and he shall direct thy paths.

Prayer is a solemn request for help or expression of thanks addressed to God. Prayer is like talking to your best friend. It's easy to talk to someone when you know they love you unconditionally. God loves you unconditionally. When we pray to God, He hears us and He loves hearing from us because He wants us to communicate with Him, like a person to person phone call. Our praying is a communication process that allows us to talk to God. Prayer is not a ritual thing or something religion but it is a direct line with heaven.

Prayer is a place where pride is abandoned, where your deepest secrets are keep, hope is lifted and where supplication is made, a place where you get help and a place where you can cast all your cares on God because He cares for you (1 Peter 5:7). When you pray, you are admitting that you need help. You adopt humility and claim dependence upon God.

Prayer is the exercise of faith and hope. It is the privilege of toughing the heart of the Father through His Son Jesus Christ. But sometimes too often we ignore prayer and do things our way. And when that happens we mess things up. But when we seek God in prayer things work out good. When we pray we should pray by faith, trusting God because He hears us. . Like I stated earlier in one of my chapters, it is impossible to please God without Faith. Anyone that comes to God must believe that He is God and that person must believe that He exists. While Daniel was in captivity he would pray to God something he did nonstop. No matter what Daniel was face with his response was the opposite of other people. Daniel was a thankful man. God's nature and how He provides was front and center in Daniel's heart, even in the midst of uncontrollable circumstances. Most people responses are usually a by-product of the rituals they have established in their lives. But Daniel made it a habit to pray with a heart of thanksgiving. Daniel knew that no matter what he went through that God was right there with him, because Daniel didn't just pray when trouble appeared in his life. He prayed every day because He depended on God. Daniel knew if he didn't communicate with God then his life would have been a living hell. Prayer wasn't a religion thing with Daniel but it was the way him and God communicated. Daniel took the scripture Proverbs 3:5 into his heart and applied it to his life. He acknowledged God in all his ways, in the good and the bad times. When life pressed in on Daniel, He pressed in on prayer because he knew that prayer changed things. For example in Daniel 6:10, Daniel had just learned that if anyone was caught praying to anyone else besides King Darius that they would be thrown into the lion's den. That's a serious pit. That day when Daniel heard about this he went home and did his usual. He opened his windows and prayed like he did any other time. Giving thanks before God, as was his custom since his early days. I don't think he did this because he felt good. I can just imagine how he felt like anyone of us would feel in overwhelming circumstances. But he didn't let how he felt keep him from praying because he knew that God would turn this bad thing around for his good so that's why he made it his business to pray like any other time. Daniel found comforter in praying to God in a time when he was feeling bad instead of finding comfort in something that he could control.

He prayed when it was against the law to pray. He was committed to prayer. Notice that it was after he knew that the law against praying to God was signed and put into effect that he continued to pray just as he had already been doing. Rather than stage a protest, he prayed. Prayer was an expression of his personal devotion to dependency on God.

He gave thanks to God and that was how he made supplication to God. Daniel was loyal to king Darius but he had a higher loyalty to God because Jesus taught that we ought always to pray and not give up (Luke18:1). Paul also said that we are to pray without ceasing (1 Thes. 5:17). And because of Daniel dedication to praying to God he was punished. The men of King Darius heard Daniel praying like they do any other day. They knew that Daniel had his window open as he prayed to God so they went by and heard him praying. They ran back and told the King that Daniel was praying. They said "King, didn't you sign a decree that every man shall ask a petition of any God or man within thirty days. If they get caught praying then they would be cast into the lion's den. Who is the person that's praying? They told the king that it was Daniel. And immediately the king got sad. He was displeased with his self. He tried everything in his power to keep Daniel from being throwing in the pit but the other men said to him, now king, a decree was signed and that no decree or statue which the king established may be changed. Right after that Daniel was brought to the king. Then they threw him in the lion den. The King didn't get any sleep that night. He felt so bad because he cared about Daniel but he couldn't change the decree. So, the next morning the king went to the lion den. He said to Daniel, servant of the living God. Is your God whom you serve able to deliver you from the lion den? Daniel, yelled to the king, my God sent his angels to shut the lions mouth so they couldn't hurt me. He said king I haven't done anything wrong to be punished for praying. He said because I put my trust in God, he was with me in the lion den. He protected me. As you can read when we pray to God he will see us through any storm just like he did Daniel. God took them same lion that should have eaten Daniel up and used them for a pillow for Daniel to lay on. God shut their mouth while Daniel was down there with them. We need to understand just like Daniel did, he knew that God was with him know matter the situation. Daniel didn't let that decree stop him from praying to God. And we shouldn't let what we are facing stop us from praying to God. Do you know that our depending on God can cause others to depend on God? The same king throw them same men in that same den that Daniel was throwing in and them lions ate them up immediately. As you can see these men didn't survive like Daniel because they weren't praying to God but they were praying to a man, a man just like them. That man couldn't deliver them.

Tool #5
Trust
Genesis 39:20-21
Joseph trusted God while he was in prison

Joseph- inspirational bible story of faith, Joseph in the bible was the overconfident younger son of Jacob. He was known to his brothers as their father's favorite. For this reason his 10 older brothers conspired against the boy and sold him to slave traders, while telling their father the boy had been mauled. Joseph had been given dreams of God's plan for his life; so with confidence and trust in God, he endured in this amazing story in Genesis. Joseph was considered dead to his family.

His father thought he was dead because Joseph brothers lied like an animal killed him. But in the mean times the slaves took him into Egypt and sold him to Potiphar, one of the Pharaoh's officers. Joseph served his master well and gained great favor. But the master's wife tried to seduce Joseph, a young man of impeccable integrity and a man who was absent from sex until marriage. After he rejected her, she went to her husband with false accusations. It resulted in Joseph's imprisonment.

It was not very difficult to stand as a faithful witness of God's goodness and glory adorned in the coat of many colors and living in the warmth and safety of his father's house but what about in the prison cell ? Joseph continued to glorify God and tell others about Him even as his own circumstances appear to be getting worse beyond hope. What did the butler and baker think (who he was sharing a cell with) about this young Hebrew and his talk about foreign God who alone possesses the answers to the question of the heart. It must not have appeared to them that God was doing much in this man's life. But through everything Joseph was going through he trusted God. Joseph praised God and gave Him glory. Nonetheless, Just like Job, Paul and Silas, Daniel, and myself , it has always been the tendency of people in the past to view a person circumstances as an indication of whether or not God's favor rest upon them. Even to this day there are those who proclaim a person's prosperity is in direct proportion to the strength of their faith. Yet, Joseph (Job, Paul and Silas, Daniel and I) certainly lacked no faith and more dire circumstances for him can scarcely be imagined. Joseph understood that those who will serve God must yield themselves to be used for His purposes and for His good pleasure and not their own. Regardless of the situation Joseph knew that God was causing all things to work in his best interests according to His own purposes (Rom. 8:28). Joseph trusted in God. Joseph's is not a faith barely hanging on as it so often feels when we face our darkest hours in life but a vivacious and exuberant trust in the living God. He remained cheerful even in the confines of incarceration is evidenced by Joseph's heartfelt concern for his temporary cell mates as he was moved by their dampened demeanor one morning after a dream they had. They looked so sad. So Joseph approached them because he knew something was bothering them. He asked why they looked so sad. They responded saying they dreamed a dream and there is no interpreter of it. Joseph response was do not interpretations belong to God? If Joseph had been in self-pity he would not have noticed the sadness on these men face but because he trusted God he didn't focus on his circumstances but instead he focused on God's promises. Joseph knew that God was working things out for his good even though he was experiencing bad events one after another. Joseph had consideration for others. Joseph could have easily badger his brothers, Potiphar's wife and Potiphar for the way they mistreated him. Instead Joseph tactfully says that he was kidnapped from the land of the Hebrews and that he didn't do anything to deserve to be in prison. He wasn't having a pity party, blaming everybody else for his trials even though in this case everybody else really was to blame. I know it hurt Joseph how everyone did him, but Joseph let God heal his pain and let God strengthen him to go in in spite of all they had done to him. Joseph kept a positive attitude. He focused on what he could do during his bad situation. Not on the things he could not do. Joseph could have thought, "What's the use of telling these two men the meaning of their dream? That won't get me any place. How can it benefit me?" But instead he didn't. He told them the interpretation of their dream. Eventually they got out of prison. Joseph told the cupbearer to remember him when he get out and show me kindness, mention me to Pharaoh and get me out of this prison. The cupbearer told Joseph that he would remember him when he got out. But he didn't. I could just picture the cupbearer giving Joseph thumbs up as he was headed out the prison door, saying, I got you friend don't worry. You will be out of here in no time!   I bet Joseph's hopes were the highest since he had been sold into slavery by his brothers. Finally, it looked like he was going to be a free man. I imagine seeing Joseph folding up his bed mattress and collecting his few things as he thought about how great it would be to see the sunshine and feel the warmth of the sun on his body and running to his father and hugging him. But again, Joseph was let down again. His high hopes were dimmed and finally extinguished as he realized the cupbearer forgot him. But he never lost hope in God. Joseph's could have easily got disappointed because his high hopes weren't met in the way he expected. He could have been despair but yet instill he had hope in God and God alone. Two years went by for Joseph. He was in his twenties, the prime in his life at that time.

I know Joseph had to fight off feelings of despair because the cupbearer had let him down. Just like everyone else had done. Yes it is so easily to be disappointed by people. And whenever you're disappointed by people, it's a short step to grow disappointed with God: and say "Lord, You can make him/her remember me. Please Lord bring my situation to that person attention so that I can get out of this (situation),for Joseph out of prison. Two long difficult years dragged by with no answer from God for Joseph. But Joseph trusted God. Disappointments like this almost always involve flaky people. This incident shows how vain it is to put your trust in people. The only consistent thing about people is that they will let you down. You can be sure that the cupbearer didn't forget in the sense of not thinking of Joseph. He probably forgot in the sense of not wanting to risk bringing up his past by mentioning Joseph to Pharaoh. Joseph could have easily moved from disappointment with this flaky man into disappointment with God. But instead Joseph processed his disappointment so that it didn't lead to crippling despair but rather to hope in God alone. During these dry two years Joseph keep believing that no matter how things looked or felt, God was with him. He knew that God vision for his life would be fulfilled. Instead of focusing on where he was and all he was going through, he focused on God promises. God had his hand on Joseph and Joseph knew it without a shadow of a doubt. God had a divine purpose for this young man. Joseph didn't know why God had chosen this path for his life until the very end, yet he never seemed to waver. God was always in control even though everything seemed out of control around Joseph. Joseph kept his eyes on God, and He used Joseph greatly. What an encouragement to us. Let God use you where you are. Let Him use you in the hard times as well as the good times.

We all deal with disappointments in life. The most difficult disappointments to deal with are when you have prayed about your situation over and over again and it seems like God doesn't hear you. You can easily get disappointed with God and stop praying. That's exactly what the devil wants you to do. It doesn't mean God doesn't hear you because you don't get what you are asking for in prayer. It simply means that God is doing things different and better for you. After all, God does have your best interest at heart. God loves you.

I know in times like this your hopes are dashed. At times like that, the first thing to do is be disappointed with God. It's easy to feel like God is playing a cruel game with you or to feel like God is punishing you. In Joseph case he could have easily got disappointed with God and said "why did he make it look like He was going to answer, only to dash my hopes?

Joseph could have easily said, " I am going to protect myself from further hurt I am going to stop praying and hoping at all." Because all I keep seeing is hopeless situations in my life" But Joseph did the opposite, he keep trusting in God because He knew that all the bad he was faced with was being worked out for his good, even when there was no hope on the horizon for Joseph. Once again God proved his presence and protection for Joseph. The prison keeper befriended him and learned of Joseph divine ability to interpret dreams. Because of earning this reputation, Joseph was called upon to interpret a dream that deeply troubled the Pharaoh. None of Pharaoh's wise consults had been able to decipher the dream. But Joseph accurately relayed the symbols in the dream to a future time of abundance that would be followed by a time of great famine. Joseph was able to interpret this dream because God revealed to him what the dream meant. This was the way God got him out of prison. God used Joseph to interpret Pharaoh's dream and that lead Joseph to be over all that Pharaoh owned. In one day Joseph went from a prisoner to prime minister of the greatest nation on the face of the earth at that time. You see it looked bad that the cupbearer didn't mention Joseph when he first got out of prison but it wasn't bad. It was a good purpose. If Joseph would have got out then, he wouldn't fulfill the vision God gave him. But praise God that Joseph kept his trust in God during all his disappointments and because of that he was filled with joy during them times. And his vision was fulfilled.

I want you to know that God's grace is always sufficient if we just will receive it. Joseph came through these trials stronger, not weaker, gentle, not bitter, because he hoped in God. Even though he was in prison, the Lord was with him. Even though the cupbearer forgot him, God never did. Joseph experienced what Paul and every other believer undergoing trails has experienced, that God's grace is sufficient for our need, if we just receive it. Your trial or your most horrible experience can become a terrific testimony but it depends on your response.

As you have read about Paul and Silas, Joseph, Daniel, Job and myself and how we have faced some of the worse storms in this life but we didn't focus on them. Instead we focused on God's word. We put our confidence solely in God and in Him alone. Not because we were strong people but because we were weak people and we knew that without depending on God we wouldn't never been able to rejoice during our most difficult times or let alone make it during them times. We needed God supernatural strength during our weakest moments. And because of God's strength during our weakest moments we made it to shore with no bumps or bruises. We made it with victory and a great message that says with God you can weather any storm.

***

I will like to leave all my readers with this; none of us is exempt from bad things happening in our lives. I need all my readers to know that this world is corrupt because of the fall of Adam in the garden. Please understand that while we are here on this earth that we all will experience something bad in our lives but it doesn't make us a bad person or a cursed person. But I leave you with some good news. With Christ, we can make it when bad things occur in our lives.

If you haven't made Jesus Christ, your Lord and Savior yet and you would like to now. Just confess with your mouth that you are a sinner and that you need Jesus Christ as your Savior. You must believe that He is the Son of God and was sent by God to take away the sins of the world, if you have asked Jesus into your heart as your Savior today. You are forgiven for your past, present and future sins. You are made righteous because Jesus Christ gave you the gift of righteousness. And you have been made brand new by the blood of Jesus. The old you is gone. But understand and know that your mind isn't made brand new. You have to renew it with the word of God daily to walk in the freedom God gave you through his Son Jesus Christ.

A Letter to a Parent from a Parent

Parents, I pray for us all because we cannot raise our kids without the help of God. We will fail and I am living proof you will. You have read my story and saw how I failed with raising my children without the help of God. Let me explain something very important to you, Jesus didn't die and rise up to give us religion or to makes us religious. He did it to give us salvation and to bring us back to God. He did it to make us right with God. Religion is people trying to find their way back to God in their own ability through their self-efforts; through trying to keep rules and rituals, and through their works. Salvation is deliverance from sin and its consequences, believed by Christians to be brought about by faith in Christ.

Parents the best thing we can give our kids is love. Not that tough love the world says they need but that love God has that will draw them to God. That love that will set them free in their mind from the devil lies.

The devil has placed lies in our children mind that God doesn't love them and that God is the reason they're in prison. He has our kids thinking there's no hope for them.

The devil even has so many of us turning our back on our children hoping to teach them a lesson. He has most of us tearing our kids down with our words, has some of us pointing out all our kids mistakes instead of pointing them to the cross where Jesus got rid of all their sins. The devil knows if we keeping pointing out their sins that we keep them in prison to sin. He doesn't want us to point out what Jesus did for them because it will set them free in their mind. Parents don't wait for your kids to change because it will never happen in their own self efforts. Instead speak God's promise over their life right now and right where they're at because that will set them free from the bondage of the devil. It is only then will you see change because where the mind goes the body will follow. I need you to know something very important; prison didn't start when the judge sentence our kids but it started in their minds. Parents please don't make the mistakes I made. Ask God every day in prayer to show you how to love your kids unconditionally because believe it or not that's going to keep your kids out of the streets looking for love or a family or a dad. Our kids need us.

I know you're probably saying Demetria, I show my kids love by working a job to keep a roof over their head, I keep clothes on their back and food on the table and I make sure I buy them the latest and greatest.

That's great parents, but we forget the most important thing and that's to give them their identity in Christ. I did all that as well as a mother but it sure didn't keep my kids out of prison. Let's not forget that we were once a child and we made a lot of mistakes and we also did a lot of things our parents didn't like. I gave my children presents instead of Christ and my presence. I raised my kids in a fatherless home while I was angry and bitter. I tore my kids apart in so many ways. It took me years to realize this because I thought I was raising my kids well but I learned the most valuable lesson and that is I raised my kids without Christ.

Prison Mom Ministry

Prison Mom is a ministry that was born out of the experiences of Demetria Williams and her two incarcerated children. True freedom is not being free from behind a jail cell, but having freedom of the mind. This ministry assists prisoners with resources and encouragement. Our ministry focuses on the people behind bars and those in the real world who are trapped behind the jail cells of their minds. Our ministry reaches to those affected by incarceration, their families, those who are looking for change and those that are affected by something devastating in their lives. We know that there is still hope no matter where you are, and that, regardless of your circumstances; you can have contentment and freedom right where you are. We understand how it feels to be shackled in your mind and how difficult it can be to find freedom. Our goal is to provide what we know is freedom in Jesus Christ through our ministry as authors.

Author Demetria experienced her own prison sentenced when she was robbed of her virginity at a young age. She was sentenced to fear, shame, guilt, darkness and experienced a strong desire for revenge. This left her feeling depressed, hopeless, angry, and shackled in her own mind.

Demetria thought her freedom began the day she told her mother what had happened, but it didn't. Even though she thought she had escaped it that day, she was still shackled in her mind, feeling unworthy, angry with God and shackled by fear. Every time she looked in the mirror, she saw pain, rage, and self-loathing. For the longest time, she was bitter and believed that suicide was the only way out of her pain. She questioned God, asking "why me?" She was trapped mentally by the trauma. No matter how hard she tried, she couldn't break free. She couldn't love her kids fully, she couldn't love herself. The turning point for Demetria began when she started replacing the lies of the devil for the truth of who she is in Christ. The truth—God's word—began to free her from the past, freeing her from the darkest days and giving her hope. Now when she looks in the mirror she sees purpose. The devil still harasses her hoping to chain her down again, but Demetria possesses her freedom by meditating on God's truth (his word). She knows freedom of the mind comes from knowing who you are in Christ. Through years of trials Demetria learned to use God's truth to triumph over any every circumstance. Demetria knows one thing for certain where ever the mind goes the body is going to follow. She knows that freedom doesn't start from behind a jail cell but it starts in the mind. She knows from her own personal experiences that incarceration didn't start for her children or other children when the judge sentenced them to many years in prison. It started in their mind and that's what landed them behind bars. Demetria backs her facts up with the word of God, He said in his word that if we sow to the flesh that we will reap fleshly results. And that's what happen in our children cases. Wrong believing causes them to follow after their flesh and that's what brought forth the consequences of prison sentence for them. Demetria knows what it's like when you are in prison to the devil lies. She knows it will lead you to do wrong things in life.

What can people expect from Prison Mom? They can expect seminars, other books and a continuous message about how to be free from the devil lies.

Also, people can expect a book club from the book Prison Mom.

Acknowledgements

I would like to thank a great and talented team of people for all their help with this book. I would like to give special thanks to Yvette Wilson Bentley and her publishing company for their great work on initially editing this project. I would like to give a special thanks to Silvie D. of Elijah Jean Editing for an awesome job on editing my book. She was a great person to work with. She was very patient with me and took her time making sure my story was at its best before I published it. She is a God-sent and an anointed editor.

Special thanks to ZMARS Designs for the great art work for my book cover,special thank you to Richard and Carol Colbeck for being a friend during this whole process. Thank you to Richard for your great artwork as well; you are awesome. Special thanks to Love Hobbs for being a great listener during this whole process and lastly a special thank you to my lovely friend who's great, English Major. She labored with me through it all; an angel sent from God. Thanks also to her lovely granddaughter and grandson. I appreciate you all. This wouldn't be possible without you all.

Most importantly a special thank you to my babies Anijah and Elijah for giving me time to myself to write this book. Thanks for not interrupting while I was writing. Anijah I know there were days that you asked yourself *"will she every finish this book because it's taking up too much of my time"*. I saw the look on your face sweetheart and I heard your mumbles under your breath. Thank you for sticking with me throughout. Mommy loves you both.

72800889R00092

Made in the USA
Columbia, SC
27 June 2017